WABI-SABI HOME

**The complete guide to finding Beauty in Imperfection and
learn all about the Japanese art of imperfection**

Noelle Gile

D2D E-book ISBN: 978-1-990836-29-9

Legal & Disclaimer

The information contained in this book and its contents is not designed to replace or take the place of any form of medical or professional advice; and is not meant to replace the need for independent medical, financial, legal or other professional advice or services, as may be required. The content and information in this book have been provided for educational and entertainment purposes only.

The content and information contained in this book has been compiled from sources deemed reliable, and it is accurate to the best of the Author's knowledge, information and belief. However, the Author cannot guarantee its accuracy and validity and cannot be held liable for any errors and/or omissions. Further, changes are periodically made to this book as and when needed. Where appropriate and/or necessary, you must consult a professional (including but not limited to your doctor, attorney, financial advisor or such other professional advisor) before using any of the suggested remedies, techniques, or information in this book.

Upon using the contents and information contained in this book, you agree to hold harmless the Author from and against any damages, costs, and expenses, including any legal fees potentially resulting from the application of any of the information provided by this book. This disclaimer applies to any loss, damages or injury caused by the use and application, whether directly or indirectly, of any advice or information presented, whether for breach of contract, tort, negligence, personal injury, criminal intent, or under any other cause of action.

You agree to accept all risks of using the information presented inside this book.

You agree that by continuing to read this book, where appropriate and/or necessary, you shall consult a professional (including but not limited to your doctor, attorney, or financial advisor or such other advisor as needed) before using any of the suggested remedies, techniques, or information in this book.

TABLE OF CONTENTS

INTRODUCTION

Wabi-sabi is a Japanese worldview that finds beauty in imperfection and transience. Hence a simple, meditative, and authentic lifestyle.

The gaze is turned inwards, beyond the external appearance, beyond the appearance. A profound aesthetic awareness enhances feelings such as melancholy and loneliness, accompanied by the serenity of liberation from the material world.

Wabi-sabi arrives in our homes because it is a philosophy of life that Westerners have begun to imitate for 20 years. Realizing that the world of consumerism was collapsing on them, they took a step back to return to the essence of life.

A life lived in search of perfection; control over nature; attachment to stability and materiality; absoluteness and clarity of concept; durability, and at times the progressive development to immortality.

It becomes a life that loves the imperfection that leads to authenticity; who loves acceptance and harmony with nature; adaptation to change and detachment from material things; relativity

1

and concept ambiguity; the changeability and cyclical development of everything.

In this way, life becomes simpler and more peaceful without inner struggles, without racing against time, but in full awareness of what it is.

This concept was also taken up in the conception of the house.

And here is what happens to the Wabi-sabi house: nothing is perfectly defined, and everything expresses its most authentic nature, leaving time to act.

The materials are natural and never subjected to excessive processing. Lime, raw earth, exposed bricks, worn woods, rough stones, raw linen, torn jute, soft wool, worn ceramic, and faded clay.

The colors and finishes are just as natural to everything. There are no fluorescent or industrial colors. No more shiny, smooth, and shiny surfaces, but rough, veined, dark, and tactile.

The shapes do the same. The naturalness of the curved and indefinite lines is far from any idea of symmetry and artificial composition.

Natural light becomes the touch of King Midas. This is considered in the organization of the spaces and the positioning of the furnishings.

Recycled materials and objects enter because time becomes a space to live.

Attention, we are far from a frikkettona, vernacular aesthetic, or a style of ethical recycling. The Wabi-sabi in the house is expressed with maniacal elegance. It adds the patina of the raw and the authentic to 21st-century minimalism. The elements are reduced to a minimum, indispensable, and positioned in a refined and non-trivial way. Spaces shrink and become darker and more private.

After changes, anxieties, and panic attacks, without knowing it, I embraced the Wabi-sabi philosophy, returning to the private and simple life that I had abandoned for a more public and furious one. I wish this change to everyone, perhaps starting right from the house.

This book will give you ideas and suggestions to adapt your home to this philosophy to improve your life both on an outward and spiritual level.

CHAPTER 1

WHAT IS WABI-SABI

Wabi: the absence of pathos, the refusal of luxury, "conscious primitivism." Sabi can be translated as "serenity," "sadness of loneliness," and "muffled colors and sounds." In the combined - and more extensive - the concept of wabi-sabi lies the lack of brilliance, naive simplicity, and the beauty of things touched by time and that carry the warmth of the multitude. Human hands- and therefore even more attractive. This concept has many shades of meaning, but none are precise and definite.

You can grasp the essence of wabi-sabi if you learn to understand life through feelings, discarding extraneous thoughts. The idea is that observing natural, changing and unique objects around us helps us connect to the real world and avoid potentially stressful distractions.

We learn to notice beauty in the most ordinary, natural way: for example, by contemplating the withering autumn leaves. Wabi-sabi gives the object a meditative value and, in this sense, becomes the practical embodiment of the philosophy of Zen Buddhism with its desire for isolation, self-control, and at the same time, inner strength and concentration.

Aesthetics of modesty

It is no coincidence that the tea master and follower of wabi-sabi Murata Juko (1422–1502) was a Zen monk. At that time, tea was a luxury item, as were ceremony accessories brought from China, ranging from exquisite to pretentious. In contrast to this fashion, Juko served tea in locally made utensils, considered coarse.

A century later, the son of the merchant Sen no Rikyu (1522–1591), who became master of the tea ceremony, continued this tradition: he made the tea house look like a peasant hut and integrated it with a garden and a stone path that leads through the park to the house. He ordered bowls from the famous master ceramist: they were shaped by hand, without a potter's wheel. Intentionally unsophisticated and imperfect, they eventually became covered with cracks, plaque, and chips.

Rikyu paid with his life for his commitment to simplicity: the overlord, whom he served, preferred magnificent receptions and precious utensils and ordered the master to commit suicide ritually. However, the tea ceremony school, founded by Rikyu, became the first in Japan and beyond its borders.

Relationships in the spirit of wabi-sabi teach you to accept another person with all his flaws but don't forget to get yours.

The essence of wabi-sabi can be summed up in three statements, says art theorist Leonard Coren, who has devoted many years to studying this principle: "Truth comes from observing nature. Greatness lives in secret and forgotten details. Beauty can come from imperfection. "

This philosophy extends to relationships, both with oneself and with other people. A relationship in the spirit of wabi-sabi teaches you to accept each other with all their flaws, but don't forget to get yours. After all, perfection can be tedious. And if we moderate our expectations and focus on the other person's perception: what he says and hears, how does he relate to the world? If we don't try to fix it, we will have more time and energy to enjoy the communication.

You can apply the same approach to yourself: I already have everything inside of me that I need to feel valued and be happy. It is enough for me to pay attention to the essentials. By avoiding the hustle and bustle and dictatorship of fashion, I can accept myself for who I am. Standard perfection and ostentatious luxury are contrasted by the uniqueness, imperfection, and modesty of wabi-sabi.

One of Leonard Coren's advice is: "Simplify everything to the point but leave the poem. Keep everything clean and uncluttered, but don't deprive it of meaning. "We, the modern world people, often need this kind of advice. The rejection of captivating beauty and excessive abundance is an ideal condition for understanding wabi-sabi, which has no clear boundaries and illuminated signs. Still, it can give an enlightened sensation of the rigorous simplicity

6

of the world around us. The three exercises we propose will help you get into the spirit of this philosophy.

Three exercises for reveal the hidden beauty

The prevailing aesthetic principles shape our gaze. But suppose we want to rediscover the freedom and freshness of feelings. In that case, we need a different approach to business: more delicate and attentive, less radical about operational changes "for the better." In the context of wabi-sabi, beauty exists beyond artificiality. As evidence of the superiority of nature over man, the consequences of random changes should not be smoothed out or canceled but, on the contrary, they should be carefully preserved.

Such as? Pay attention to the imperfections of things and people. The faded folds of old fabric, the beauty of dry leaves or a falling flower, the charm of an older man's smile and the pattern of wrinkles on his face, the dance of dust in a ray of light - all this is beautiful., and therefore worthy of a lot of attention.

Distinguish the shades of emotions and enjoy them. When we enter a problematic situation, stressed or simply not very well, it is helpful to contact some object imbued with the spirit of wabi-sabi, which, according to the definition, can "excite a feeling of slight sadness and spiritual thirst in us." It helps remind us of the illusory nature of permanence and perfection, the ephemeral nature of problems and worries, and that no one can conquer time.

Such as? Wandering around the house, touching your favorite clothes, opening an old book, picking up a glass of water, stopping at some wabi-sabi object, feeling its weight, shape, and texture. What attracts you to this topic, and why is it pleasant? What memories and feelings does it evoke? Nostalgia, slight sadness, joy? By understanding this, you will feel more confident and be able to discern a whole range of different shades in your emotions.

Choose what makes us happiest. Recognize Primary Needs The best way to know yourself and get closer to your uniqueness. Wabi-sabi does not involve self-denial and forced minimalism but only a conscious choice according to one's inner essence.

Such as? For example, make a list of activities that bring you joy. Think about what exactly they are pleasant for you and what deep characteristics of your personality they correspond to. Assign these activities serial numbers 1 to 6, and ask yourself: do you spend enough time on them - and during each day?

CHAPTER 2
THE CHARACTERISTICS OF ZEN
AESTHETICS

The modern study of a Japanese aesthetic in the Western sense began only a little over two centuries ago. Japanese aesthetics now embrace various ideals, some of which are traditional while others are modern and sometimes influenced by other cultures.

Shinto is considered to be the source of Japanese culture. Its emphasis on the concern for nature and the character of ethics and its celebration of the landscape sets the tone for Japanese aesthetics. Nonetheless, Japanese aesthetic ideals are predominantly influenced by Japanese Buddhism. 5) In the Buddhist tradition, all things evolve and dissolve into nothingness. This "nothing" is not a space. Instead, it is a space of potentiality. 6) If we take the seas as representatives of potential, then everything is like a wave that comes from it and returns to it. There are no continuous waves. There are no ideal waves. Even at its peak, a wave is never complete. Nature is viewed as a living entity that must be admired and appreciated. This love of nature has been at the heart of many

Japanese aesthetic ideals, "arts," and cultural elements. In this regard, the concept of "art" (or its conceptual equivalent) differs significantly from Western traditions (see Japanese art).

Wabi and Sabi refer to a careful approach to daily life. Over time their meanings have overlapped and are converted to unify in Wabi-sabi, the traditional aesthetic, the beauty of "imperfect, impermanent and incomplete" things. 6) Things in bud or things in decay are more evocative of the wabi-sabi of things in full bloom because they suggest the transience of things. As things come and go, they present signs of their coming and going, and these signs are considered beautiful. Beauty is an altered state of awareness and can be seen in the mundane and the simple. Nature's signatures can be so subtle that only a quiet mind and a cultivated eye can discern them. 7) In Zen philosophy, there are seven aesthetic principles for attaining Wabi-Sabi. 8

Shin'ichi Hisamatsu (1889-1980, Zen master and distinguished professor of religion at the University of Tokyo, decided to write down the characteristics that distinguish the actual Zen aesthetic from all other things inspired by this philosophy. He defined seven attributes with which to describe what Zen is, based on the ways of expressing itself of the formless self, which, precisely because they represent this undivided entity, coexist without being able in any way to be in contrast with each other; we will be amazed at how each time, when the object or the phenomenon we are examining is truly Zen, identifying even just one of them also brings with it the discovery of all the others: it can therefore be said that these seven characteristics are interdependent, that is, they are like many faces of a prism.

The first is fukinsei, which in Japanese means asperity and asymmetry and is an aesthetic concept, opposite to our ideal of classical beauty, which we find in all Far Eastern art, where the principle controls the harmony of a composition is not nonexistent but simply not regular. Discovering how a work of art manages to be perfectly balanced without having to resort to geometric parameters and being able to see beauty in what is crooked, incomplete, odd, broken, and inexact are experiences that approach spontaneity and randomness of nature, provoke a much more quiet enjoyment than that aroused by recognizing in the world around us those abstract forms that our rationality has studied how to measure.

The second characteristic is kanso, or sobriety, which, as we have seen before about the term Wabi, is one of the qualities that arouse greater appreciation in the Japanese soul since this is extremely simple and solid. Natural beauty, everyone succeeds, identifying himself in what he sees, withdrawing into himself and on the one hand feeling a great sense of harmony and union with the whole universe, on the other perceive the vitality, the incredible tension within apparently still and composed things. Furthermore, with sobriety, we also mean that simplification leaves room for imagination, the synthesis of an item or a concept, achieved using the least possible number of elements; this poetics of absence is also a characteristic of the Far Eastern soul in general.

In third place, we find Koko, a concept that we translate as "austere dignity," which indicates the elegant beauty of decadence, which we can see in things that are old, cracked, cracked, broken, eaten by worms, with patches, scars, wrinkles. Austere dignity is achieved only when the work is dried to its essence if clarity comes from spontaneous purity. This grave beauty brings out the rough charm and consistency of maturity. As Antoine de Saint - Exupéry (perhaps) said, "perfection is not achieved when there is nothing more to add, but nothing more to take away."

Shizen, which means naturalness, is one of the fundamental characteristics of Zen aesthetics since it is the reflection of the creative process: the creation of a work of art whose content is the enlightened vision of existence must take place without purpose, in the total absence of a will, of the self and any kind of deception; everything that is produced being in this state of grace will consequently be similar to the spontaneity of nature, wonderfully harmonious, fresh, free, fluid. However, it must be emphasized that this naturalness is not identical to Western concepts of innate, naive, or instinctive. Still, it is instead a very particular way, that is spiritual, of using a technique that we have learned by studying with commitment and effort: to achieve something that can be defined shizen, after having achieved absolute mastery of the method, we must learn to concentrate all our physical and psychic forces, to relax, forget ourselves and let creation happen spontaneously, since our ego no longer exists as such, but it has merged with the thing we are making and with everything around us. The naturalness of a work lies in showing its intentional character and purpose without being artificial or insincere. Hisamatsu writes: "Naturalness emerges when the artist penetrates deeply into what he is creating that he cancels all conscious effort." To achieve this value, constant practice, profound knowledge of the technique, and extraordinary concentration are required.

Eugen's fifth characteristic is the impenetrable depth and withheld secrecy of things, which we have already described in the previous paragraph. Yugen could be translated as reverberation. The echo principle highlights how often suggestion is much more potent than full manifestation. The work must be deep and subtle. It must stimulate the imagination, the question, the reflection, rather than immediately run out and stagnate. User curiosity is a powerful push to action, as the designer can exploit such.

The sixth is daisuzoku, freedom from any attachment, the abandonment of any form, the bonds that force us to the conventional world, ideas, feelings, and overcome any dualism. "If you see a Buddha, kill him!" is one of the many irreverent maxims of Zen that, in search of a total coherence that admits no exceptions, when he says that we must overcome all attachment, he also means that towards the idea of Buddha.

When the routine is broken, creativity and innovation emerge. This principle describes the feeling of awe and energy that arises when one goes beyond the commonly accepted conventions and rules. It is necessary to adopt what in the Zen doctrine is called "beginner's mind": the attitude to take nothing for granted, to face every problem with a fresh mind, to ask the most basic questions to overcome the usual ways of acting, and reasoning.

Zen aesthetics' seventh and final characteristic is seijaku, which means silence, stillness, and serene composure. These qualities serve to calm and relax the observer's soul and come from the state of deep concentration and the meditation of the creator. However, we must not imagine that this feeling of tranquility is due to contingent factors such as an absolute silence or immobility of things; on the contrary, the effect of seijaku is much more evident and powerful where we will be able to perceive the stillness in the movement and the silence in the noise since it means that we are in a state of mind where nothing can disturb our inner peace.

This principle presents the artist who becomes one with the surrounding reality, imperturbable. The true essence of creative energy can only be found in a similar state of active calm, solitary tranquility gained through meditative practice. And it is precisely in the most chaotic and frantic moments, that this value manages to show itself with more significant impact, as the Zen saying suggests: "With the cry of the bird, the mountain becomes even quieter."

"The others are also contained in each of these seven unitary traits. Of course, it is possible that - according to the current situation - a certain section stands out on the others and that the others pass in the background,» writes Hisamatsu. "But these essential traits do not exist in isolation each for himself; instead, they are perfectly fused and form a unitary whole.»

Here is the crucial point: if assimilated and employed as a cohesive set of design principles, these concepts can put us on the right path and guide our efforts towards that ideal of minimalism that resides in the surprising impact of simplicity.

Remaining faithful in everything to Zen philosophy, Shin'ichi Hisamatsu expresses these seven characteristics positively and negatively.

Fukinsei is also mu-ho, no rule, absence of any ordered organization.

Kanso is Mutsu, which is not complex, without too many directions or interpretations, and tension towards overcoming dualism.

At the same time, Koko is mu-i, which means indefinite, since what has extinguished in itself every link with the senses has finally come to be pure essence without form, precisely indefinable.

Shizen finds its negative form in mushin, no heart or mind (the word shin in Japanese has both of these meanings, which further demonstrates the enormous underlying diversity between this culture and the European one), i.e., not forced by thoughts and emotions but unconditional, without purpose, without will.

Yugen is also mutei, bottomless, infinite.

Daisuzoku is mu- ge, without hindrance, not conditioned by the distinction between me and not-me, devoid of oppositions, internal contradictions, and obstacles.

Finally, the other side of seijaku is mu-do, which means numbness, being devoid of any emotion, be it discomfort or happiness, since any form of involvement implies anxiety, which disturbs the absolute stillness of formlessness.

These, therefore, according to Zen, are the seven characteristics of the formless self, of Buddha-nature, of the real essence of Truth. For this reason, they define the contours of the aesthetics relating to this philosophy, which is not limited to being an artistic criterion. But it involves the entire existence of every human being.

To live in line with this religion or philosophy, one should not limit oneself to using these directives to create a painting, a garden, ikebana, a haiku, work in ceramics, or a theater piece. No: following the Zen aesthetic even in actions such as the tea ceremony and the art of the sword should serve as a starting point to apply it to every gesture of daily life, to be sure to do everything correctly (a fundamental idea for Japanese culture, which also has a word on purpose to define this concept, that is kata and in harmony with the flow of the universe.

CHAPTER 3

"MONO NO AWARE"

W hen the cherry trees begin to bloom in Japan, the event is celebrated by a customer with a thousand-year history. The Hanami, which in Japanese means "admire the flowers," consists precisely in observing and enjoying the beauty of sakura (cherry blossoms) by organizing picnics and outdoor walks. This ancient tradition is closely linked to Buddhism and Zen philosophy: the cherry blossom is, in fact, the symbol of the transience of human life and the impermanence of reality. The incredible show offered by the cherry trees in bloom lasts only a few days, it is fleeting like everything that surrounds us, but it is precisely this that makes it so fascinating and unique. The Hanami best expresses the Japanese aesthetic concept of "mono no aware. "

If we wanted to translate it into words, "mono no aware" can be defined as the pathos of things, a feeling of emotional participation in existence. It indicates the sense of nostalgia that seizes us after having admired something beautiful but fleeting, which we know will not last long. The term is the union of two words: "mono," which means "things," and "aware," which initially indicated the 'exclamation of amazement towards a natural subject. Subsequently, "aware" took on the meaning of "compassion," "pity," and "sadness." Therefore, the "mono is no aware" is that feeling of melancholy that derives from the appreciation of incredible beauty and the vast awareness of its transience. It is the observation that becomes feeling. The poignant loneliness of beauty, what in one moment is, and the next moment is no more.

Impermanence: beauty is in change

However, beyond the resulting sadness, there is also essential teaching of oriental wisdom behind this concept: the impermanence and transience of things make them unique and enhance their beauty. If the cherry trees were always in bloom, they would certainly lose much of their charm. Furthermore, the awareness of impermanence in the Buddhist vision is fundamental to adapting to the unpredictability of events and the ephemeral nature of things. Much human suffering comes from the inability to accept detachment, change, and end. But life is an implacable flow of events, of beginnings and endings. Taking it allows us to understand that there is no need to resist and that if everything is temporary and fleeting, worrying about it becomes useless. Because this moment is brief, we must learn to enjoy it fully.

The mono no aware finds its maximum literary expression in one of the main works of Japanese literature, the Genji Monogatari. The novel revolves around the story of the emperor's son, and the speech he delivers when he is close to death is perhaps the most representative of the "pathos of things" of which the work is the symbol:

"I don't complain about a destiny that I share with flowers, insects, and stars. In a universe where everything passes like a dream, we would not forgive ourselves for lasting forever. It does not pain me that things, beings, and hearts are perishable since part of their beauty is made up of this calamity. What bothers me is that we are unique... Other women will be in bloom, smiling like the ones I loved, but their smiles will differ. Other hearts will break under the weight of unbearable love, but their tears will not be our tears. Hands moist with desire will continue to intertwine under the almond trees in bloom, but the same shower of petals never falls twice on human happiness."

We introduce this concept because, as we will see later in the Wabi-sabi design, a fundamental role is given by the presence of plants.

CHAPTER 4

FUKINSEI, REALISTIC BEAUTY: WHEN HARMONY IS WELCOMING IMPERFECTIONS

Fukinsei comes from Japan and indicates a real philosophical concept rather than a single untranslatable term. The word Fukinsei refers, in fact, to Japanese aesthetics and to that type of harmonic beauty that comes exclusively from asymmetry, imperfection, and diversity. A concept is distant from the ideal of classical beauty based on proportions falling within idealized canons. The term Fukinsei means asperity, asymmetry, a principle found in all oriental art where harmony is essentially irregularity. Geometric parameters, measurements, and proportions are banned; the natural beauty in Japanese culture is to grasp the pleasantness in what is not optimal. Seeing beauty in an out-of-proportion, the crooked, inaccurate figure is precisely the purpose of the Fukinsei philosophy.

This awareness helps men to approach spontaneity, chance, and nature in all its forms; beauty is realism in nature, and what the natural order of things offers is not governed by mathematical models, but by pure chance, by the creative power that assembles itself and is perfect in all its most minor inaccuracies. The deception, calculation, and measure is packaged perfection; what is beautiful will be beautiful despite and above all, thanks to its inaccuracies.

Art as a possibility

The concept of perfection, as well as that of immortality and infinity, is logically beyond the reach of any human being. Precisely for this reason, the philosophy of Fukinsei (不均 斉) wants to convey a type of art in which everyone can reflect and recognize themselves. Asymmetry generates change, movement, and dynamism instead of symmetrical balance synonymous with stasis and immobility, as it is chained to non- transformation. We all transform in our lives, and we need to keep this in mind. Irregularity is valued when the work is not entangled in the obsessive search for perfection and goes beyond symmetrical exactness. This characteristic is peculiar to the incomplete and, translated into our field, can consist of a dynamic balance of asymmetrical shapes or in the choice of a design process that encourages active participation (co-design) by users.

CHAPTER 5

JAPANESE AESTHETICS IN DESIGN

We could sum up Japanese interior design in the word Zen

Whether you live in an apartment, country cottage, or 1970s building, everyone can benefit from these Japanese style tips.

1) A Japanese style room is Multifunctional and flexible

One reason people love Japanese interior design is its vast space improvement. And who doesn't love making their home feel bigger and airier? This is because many traditional Japanese homes embrace open-plan living areas.

This popular space-enhancing style is an excellent option if you're a city dweller who understands the desirability of ground space! Combining your kitchen, dining area, and living room into one ample space will give you more space to play and create a great, friendly space where you can host and share your time with others.

2) Japanese interior design is in tune with nature and natural light

The rise of famous and incredible cultures, such as the cottage come trend, brings the outdoors inside and makes us feel less claustrophobic in our homes. However, cottagecore is maximalist and not popular with those who like a clean, minimalist look. Japanese design responds to this need.

shizen" philosophy is a principle that recognizes harmony between people and nature and underpins many Japanese furniture design methods that often use bamboo and light woods. Thanks to this philosophy, many designers also use nature to honor the world they live in.

Large windows for smooth, natural light

First, large windows and sliding doors are crucial to allowing natural light to flood the room.

Choose large sheet metal windows to maximize light and connect with natural fiber carpets and furniture outdoors.

One of the main reasons many Japanese opt for paper blinds is because they place a lot of importance on privacy. These paper screens or "Shoji" let in light but keep prying eyes out.

You could add a sliding glass door, perhaps with a glass panel in a wooden frame.

Natural and sustainable fibers

All Japanese homes reflect their surroundings and frequently use sustainable materials mixed with natural fibers.

Wood, bamboo, and rattan are common materials used for various interior characteristics. The inserts, walls, frames, mezzanines, and screen grilles are usually made of natural wood such as cypress and red pine. Wood adds texture, serenity, and sophistication to your space.

The flooring is either wood or gray stone tiles, and most of the walls are replaced by screens covered with matte paper. This design ends up in a very neutral natural color palette.

Water features and plants

Plants are one of the most common ways to incorporate the outside into the home. However, if you want to look Japanese, stick to plants with an oriental feel.

Plants are another excellent way to bring nature into your Japanese-style interior. In a Japanese-inspired interior, a bonsai tree is a standard feature. A variety of green plants rooted indoors can also be considered. Dumbcanes, aloe vera, palm trees, and orchids are plants that you can use. The plants can also be potted or hung, which adds elegance.

Bringing water features indoors is always a good idea to get a zen-like space in your home. In addition to physical water features, an oriental water-themed mural is another way to add a water element to the house.

3) Minimalism is fundamental

Because of its emphasis on "Shibui": simple beauty, detail, and a love of natural materials, contemporary Japanese design is one of the great versions of today's minimalism.

The Japanese consider the most basic form of simplicity to be a form of luxury. Contemporary, simple, clean-lined furniture from this world often has incredibly intricate engineering with intricate joinery.

Decluttering goes hand in hand with a modern Japanese home. Just follow the famous Japanese organization consultant Marie Kondo to find out!

Austerity, minimalism, and an appreciation of memorabilia and traditions survive in a unique amalgam that adapts technology and modernism to fit into an already established aesthetic and not the other way around.

Japanese minimalism is aesthetic but, above all, functional.

4) Choose neutral colors

In close connection with nature, the most common color schemes found in Japanese interior design are heavily influenced by the outside.

CHAPTER 6

THE SEVEN PRINCIPLES OF WABI-SABI

As we have seen, the Wabi-sabi is a philosophy of life that sees beauty in imperfections. Pursuing perfection generates unnecessary stress and anxiety as we should be satisfied with the importance of being unique, with our defects, which are also a virtue.

According to the Zen monks, this philosophy consists of 7 practices:

- Finding the beauty in the underrated. Known as Shibumi.

- Enhance the subtle details. Yugen.

- To be free. Datsuzoku.

- Live with simplicity. Kanso.

- Act naturally, without pretensions. Shizen.

- Appreciate the asymmetry and irregularity. Fukinsei.

- Make tranquility your lifestyle. Seijaku.

How is Wabi-Sabi applied to decoration?

This way of life has similar principles to minimalism, as it values everything we have and reminds us that we don't need to want more and more. It is about knowing how to differentiate between what you want and what is necessary.

It is the antonym of the consumer society where duration loses value and importance is given to impulse purchases. For example, an excellent example of a Wabi-Sabi would be an old plate that was broken but was repaired by joining its pieces together.

Appreciate the beauty of what surrounds us, its history, the sentimental value of each object, and the authenticity that lies in the modest and imperfect. Nothing is permanent, and the old should be appreciated rather than rejected.

Wabi-Sabi so much?

Because it is a sustainable lifestyle that enhances natural materials, furniture, and decorations that are handed down from generation to generation and clarifies how important it is to find objects that last and are functional.

This is where traditional craftsmanship and techniques, solid wood, and natural fibers come into play, allowing the creation of unique and unrepeatable pieces with a value that goes far beyond the object itself.

Wabi-Sabi means touching the ground with your feet, remembering who you are, and forgetting what society asks of you. Breathe, think about what's essential and evaluate your imperfections and those of others.

CHAPTER 7
WABI-SABI IN FURNITURE

Until a few years ago, everyone was focused on hygge style, that is, on the furnishing of a Scandinavian-style house, a design characterized by creating simple interior spaces without neglecting every comfort. Recently, however, the spotlight has been on the aesthetics of Wabi-sabi, the new frontier of interior design that comes directly from Japan.

Enough with the obsession with order; true beauty lies in imperfection. It is the philosophy of wabi-sabi, which has very ancient origins but can still be applied everywhere, in life and the home.

The wabi-sabi philosophy, or the beauty of imperfection

Ancient Japanese art is to mend broken cups or plates with gold. That is proof of how much the Asian people love highlighting the imperfection of things.

Well, this is also reflected in wabi-sabi.

The wabi-sabi constitutes a vision of the Japanese world, or aesthetic, founded on accepting the transience of things. A simple translation of wabi-sabi could be sad beauty, but the word does not have a proper translation. If anything, it is the association of two terms, Wabi, and Sabi, which indicate living in harmony with nature, making the most of what little you have, and the cold, poverty, or being "withered." Towards the fourteenth century, Wabi began to identify rustic simplicity, freshness, or silence, applied to both natural and artificial objects, or even elegance without ostentation. Furthermore, the term can also refer to oddities or defects generated in the construction process, adding uniqueness and elegance to the object. Sabi is now connoted as the beauty or serenity that accompanies the advancement of age, the acceptance of the slow and inevitable passage of time, and the moment in which the life of objects and its impermanence are highlighted by patina and wear. Or any visible repairs.

Today, imperfect beauty is applied, for example, to the house's design, where chaos, at least apparent, has taken the place of clean and tidy environments.

They can be created that make you feel good, authentic pieces because they are imperfect. The wabi-sabi imperfection is not the "artificial" one of shabby chic: here, every scratch and burn to sign the inevitable passage of time.

The house becomes authentic and fully lived, and you are no longer ashamed not to make the bedroom as soon as you get up or order books and newspapers. The tables and cutting boards become lived-in objects, with marks and veins, unfinished ceramics, and raw fabrics that have not always passed under the care of the iron; the best pieces of furniture are handcrafted, and the table is weathered.

Those who have always hated using unmatched glasses and plates for their guests can permanently free themselves from the terror of judgment, and those who hastened to hide crumpled clothes in the room can instead leave them on display on the sofa. Does that seem too much? Start gradually, preferring natural fabrics to silk and country herbs in vases instead of tulips.

To honor the passage of time, durable furniture and materials to be exposed to the elements of the passing years are fundamental, such as wood, wool, clay, bamboo, linen, and stone. Even the colors recall nature, such as the gray of the rock, the blue of the sea, and the green of the sequoia.

In reality, the wabi-sabi style is not an absolute search for simplicity but a way to combine this with beauty, which should not be sacrificed, but only interpreted differently. Not necessarily as perfection and order. Philosophy invites us to rethink our concept of "essential," to be also applied to the home, which must be filled not (only) with beautiful but functional objects and which, above all else, make you feel good.

Are you ready to live without the obsession with order, or do you prefer a slow approach to philosophy not to be traumatized by the beautiful chaos of wabi-sabi?

CHAPTER 8
SOME BASIC RULES TO FOLLOW

Japanese furniture is a must these days; it can make spaces seem more significant and help create elegant and sober housing solutions, obtaining beautiful and designed environments but also convenient and functional. Bringing a breath of Japan into your home is not difficult. However, there are rules to follow. Let's see what they are.

When dealing with open or confined spaces, this type of furniture expands the areas and organizes them thanks to its simplicity and essentiality.

The characteristics of this style are exact and include clean and regular lines, a minimal design, the use of natural materials, and sober colors. The watchwords are modern minimalism, an approach seasoned with natural touches given by wood and greenery, enriched by elements typical of Asian culture. The simplicity of this furniture is also a functional and practical solution.

We could sum up Japanese interior design in the word Zen

Use furniture and accessories with clean and essential lines.

Choose low furniture solutions, almost adherent to the floor.

I prefer sober color ranges, preferably neutral colors.

Insert natural materials using them in furniture, furnishings, and carpets.

Arrange the furnishings orderly and rigorous without bringing them too close.

Enrich the rooms with elements typical of Asian cultures, such as particular paintings, tea sets, bonsai, statues, paper lamps, and other furnishings.

Avoid knick-knacks and excessive knick-knacks, eliminating the superfluous such as paintings and carpets.

I prefer windows through which natural light can penetrate.

If necessary, divide the space without closing it, but simply use shoji panels in rice paper or dividers, for example, with typical Japanese decorations (such as orchids or cherry branches).

Create small Zen corners with rocks, fountains, and plants.

To furnish the house with a Japanese design, it is essential to take care of each environment in a specific way, ensuring that the distinctive elements of the Japanese style are present in all the house rooms. We summarize them; then, we will deepen them in various chapters.

Japanese furniture for the living area

The living room is where guests are welcomed and where most of the time is spent. The Japanese furnishings will essentially be the

TV cabinet, the sofa, and a coffee table. Therefore, the room should appear almost empty, devoid of all those decorations and objects that are not useful.

The various pieces of furniture should have simple lines, preferably geometric and square, resulting in a structure that is almost touching the ground. A typical feature of the oriental world is, in fact, that of sitting on the floor, on cushions or mats. Instead of the usual carpet, it is better to choose mats in natural material or tatami mats. On the other hand, the sofa should be large and straightforward, low, and almost adherent to the floor.

Japanese style bedroom

The modern style is very close to Japanese essentiality, so the choice on the market is extensive. This is also evident in the bedroom, for example. The futon is now very easily found in various colors and patterns with a shape very similar to the traditional Japanese style bed.

The shades should be natural wood or opt for white as much as possible. The rules are the same as those followed for the stay: therefore, those elements that are too many must be eliminated.

Japanese style kitchen decor

To set up a Japanese-style kitchen, the principles to be respected are the same that is essentiality, minimalism, and functionality, favoring natural light and chromatic harmonization. An optimal solution is kitchen furniture with sliding doors to replicate traditional Japanese furniture design.

We can decorate the walls with Japanese-style wallpaper with references to oriental culture, or for a less invasive option, you can prefer stencils. A touch of real Japan is the Japanese lanterns used as skylights, or you can use bamboo chandeliers and the inevitable bonsai.

How to Apply 8 Wabisabi Styles to Your Life

The wabi-sabi style, when used at work and in life, can seem complicated at first glance. For example, when creating an interior in the style of wabi-sabi, the main thing is to meet the following requirements:

Get rid of unnecessary things in the house. Anything you haven't used for a year is considered excessive. They steal your time and energy to take care of them, but, in reality, you don't need such items. We will see in a separate chapter how to practice decluttering.

Don't buy or bring anything extra into the house. This means not purchasing goods under the influence of emotions or because everyone has "this item" now.

Don't expose too many things. Let it be just one or two things you care about.

Do not try to fill the whole room with things, but, on the contrary, rely on free space.

Tidy things up that are filled with a pleasant "story" for you to emphasize their flavor.

Focus on objects made of natural materials, perhaps caused by a local craftsman, or objects that speak of your history, something that comes from your hometown.

In life, the wabi-sabi philosophy is expressed in the love for simplicity, for all that is natural. It's about functionality, not a demonstration of luxury. For example, using the wabi-sabi style in her life and work, Jessica Alba founded a company that produces natural cosmetics for children's skincare.

And Robert De Niro, also a follower of Japanese philosophical principles, when he finished the 630-meter Greenwich Hotel, used natural materials for the area in which the building is located: stone and wood. The building has a more captivating and familiar aesthetic.

Another critical aspect of the wabi-sabi lifestyle is that this "path of simplicity" does not require a lot of investment. Almost anyone can implement it in their lives. For example, following this worldview, to cover the floor in an apartment, you can choose not a luxurious and expensive walnut but a more common pine and perceive its natural pattern not as an asymmetry but as harmonious natural beauty.

Also, your favorite knitted sweater can be tidied up with the help of stylish patches, and the cracks in the bathroom tiles can be filled in with beautiful paint. As a result, things will be preserved, you will not have to buy anything new, and their native warmth will warm your heart for a long time.

Learn to enjoy what you have to simplify your life, and you will see that the hustle and bustle will leave you, and you will become much calmer and happier.

CHAPTER 9

WABI-SABI DESIGN

Wabi-sabi- style interior initiated the well-known European "minimalism." It will not be easy for European municipalities to get used to such an interior immediately.

The wabi-sabi design trend is not focused on luxury or exuberance; it is designed to seek Truth, meaning, and beauty much deeper than the surface. The wabi-sabi style is often found in Japanese hotels, in the more expensive rooms. This indicates how much the Japanese appreciate the genuineness, sincerity, and simplicity that the wabi-sabi "absorbed" into itself. Now, even in modern European interiors, you can see the motifs of this style. They gladly decorate the whole house with antique materials under wabi-sabi, giving new life to worn-out things with their unique history.

What does wabi-sabi mean?

If you translate the phrase " wabi -sabi," it will sound like modesty, simplicity, and calm. Wabi is unpretentious simplicity, while Sabi is harmony in solitude. This style represents Japanese beauty and sophistication. It is expressed not only in one of the interior styles; it is a whole philosophy and lifestyle of the Japanese. The peculiarity of the wabi-sabi design trend is to show that chaos reigns over precision and judgment. This is expressed in the asymmetry and irregularity of the lines. Wabi-sabi wants to show us the good side of an imperfect world.

The designers tried to show us the very texture of the materials without hiding them under a layer of unnatural colors. Those internal details that declare their novelty are not chosen; the more "seasoned" things with a long history are preferred.

Therefore, Japanese people value space very much and do not take up all the free space. This is one of the main features of this design.

Wabi-sabi colors

Natural and light shades should prevail. To create an antique interior, it is best to use white, beige, milky, gray, and brown colors. The off-white color is trendy. It is he who can so accurately convey the mood of wabi-sabi design. It is often used to decorate walls, floors, or furniture. The wabi-sabi design trend includes a continuous connection with nature. To do this, dark woods are actively used in the interior, which brightly contrasts against the background of light walls. All materials used in wabi-sabi are tested to be left smooth and unprocessed. The same applies to wooden surfaces, which in no case should be painted in unnatural colors, but only slightly hidden by the paint. This creates a unique interior in your home and maintains a special atmosphere.

Wall texture

As we have already said, the main thing in this style is simplicity, non-invasiveness, and naturalness. This applies to the small details of the wabi-sabi design and the wall decoration itself. The best materials will be stone, wood, brick, metal, or concrete. No matter what it will be, the main thing is that they can "talk" about themselves. A suitable material for wall decoration will be a brick painted in light colors. In no case should the house cry out to its newness and luxury, just restraint and modesty? The stylistic trend is somewhat similar to the rustic style.

Moreover, you can see the clear motifs of its design in wabi-sabi. But, unlike the rustic, the latter is fraught with the philosophy and mystery of Japanese beauty—a minimum of finishing, polishing, varnishing, and a maximum of naturalness and imperfection. Wabi-sabi does not recognize artificiality and elegance: everything should be light and discreet.

Wabi-sabi furniture

Furniture for this style also needs to be selected specially. When choosing it, you should pay attention to natural and natural materials. The table doesn't have to be perfect; it can look unfinished and asymmetrical. Wabi-sabi interior design often uses DIY furniture, which further emphasizes the particularity of the style. The rough stone that covered the fireplace, the rough surface of the wood, the "worn" look, and the strange shapes of benches, chairs, and tables: this is what distinguish Japanese interiors. But, even though wabi-sabi implies old and worn things, that doesn't mean that modern notes can't be added. New technologies go well with the imperfect Japanese style. They have learned to combine modernity with antiquity, adding fresh notices to the classic wabi-sabi style.

Floor materials

The best materials for a wabi-sabi floor would be wood or concrete. There is no fine parquet, carpet, or bright tiles, just restraint and simplicity. If it is a concrete floor, it must be well sanded. The material may look shabby and old - this will be the basis for the entire interior design in the style of wabi-sabi. If you like a tree, it should also show its ancient history with its appearance. Modern hardware stores offer us a large selection of various types of floor coverings made to match the interior of wabi-sabi. They will be good helpers in creating this unique design.

Lighting

Wabi-sabi's interior lighting philosophy is similar to Scandinavian-style interior lighting - soft, muted, and diffused light. The interior of Wabi-sabi inherited this principle from the lighting of the Japanese teahouse - Chashitsu, which was purposely built with windows on the north side and next to which trees grew that spread even more light. (You can read more about the effect of orientation to the cardinal points inside).

Storage spaces

All these things come together, guided by the principle of

"timelessness." It shouldn't be clear from within which century it belongs. Therefore, it is not allowed that a plasma TV hung in plain sight in such an interior or there was a high-tech iMac.

How do we solve such a problem? After all, we are talking about modern interiors and modern people. Now there is no problem; order a built-in wardrobe in the joinery for the entire height of the wall. Raw panels can be taken as facades. Inside there will be storage space and a retractable TV. You can even do an electric drive with remote control. And the cabinet doors will open by pressing them. It is cute simple technology widely used in kitchen fronts. Imagine that not the photo below is not a single block of planks but three doors on hidden hinges—an entirely feasible design.

In the end, if the area of the room allows, you can make a separate storage room for things, which in the interior can be relatively modern.

And as for the computer - remember, this is conscious modesty, so just a laptop that you keep on your knees while you work, and then take it off so as not to be noticeable.

As you can see, even at first glance, the exotic interior of our country can be recreated without special financial or temporary costs. After all, sushi and sashimi have taken root in our country, so why not make Japanese interiors?

The most important thing is that nothing catches the eye with its unearthly beauty and perfection. On the other hand, the surrounding things can be seen with pleasure, thus immersing oneself in the real space around you instead of running somewhere. Part or dig into your phone. The style should be so subtle that it is not visible.

Accessories are simple, modest, and nostalgic elements: ceramics and stones.

Simple doesn't mean cheap, especially for accessories. It is not so easy to choose the correct details for this style in the modern world. Choose the most natural and possibly unfinished. As you know, naturalness costs a lot of money. Various vases, pots, bowls, figurines, engravings, etc., are welcome in the design. The main thing is natural materials, such as clay, stone, metal, or wood. Choose handmade items, especially dishes. The various plants that will bring your home to life are not without importance. Pots for them are also better to choose from clay.

Style wabi-sabi is not governed by fashion but by the ability of things to tell their story. Nothing extra in it that can distract attention. Wabi-sabi was created for comfort and solitude so that a person can put his thoughts in order.

But don't be mad if Wabi -Sabi's inside isn't within your reach. You need to be very creative and resourceful so that the house can be decorated with your own hands. National motifs will add uniqueness to this style. It is not necessary to adopt everything from the Japanese. "Minimalism" can be created on your own. Making rooms with the right colors is half the problem; the important thing is to create the correct details. Try looking for old clay pots, cups, and plates in the attic. They will become indispensable accessories in your home. If you don't find them, you can now easily buy an ordinary clay pot and decorate it with antique spray cans of various colors. There will also be multiple wooden baskets and chests. Turn on the fantasy, and you will be successful!

The beauty of purity, transition, and imperfection of Wabi-sabi is at odds with the definition of classical Western beauty, which emphasizes perfection, durability, monumentality, and materialistic obsession. Incorporating the Wabi-sabi philosophy doesn't mean hiring an interior designer, becoming a Japanese culture expert, or living like a Buddhist monk.

Adopting the Wabi-sabi philosophy requires a shift in your perspective. By removing the obsession with material possessions, you should be able to create a happier home where you feel more satisfied.

You don't have to let yourself be overwhelmed by runaway shopping to decorate your home; you don't need anything new to change your home. Japanese philosophy values nature, so pay attention to the materials you bring home. Wood, stone, and metal elements are predominant, aesthetically pleasing, and age well.

These are some accessories you already own and have never appreciated! Choose based on the principles of functionality, minimalism, and simplicity. Search the kitchen drawer, where it waits to find some old rusty knife or some other iron, brass, or copper object. Their imperfections tell a story of years and years of use. You may come across a chipped vase, container, bowl, or flowerpot in your basement or attic. All the signs of wear or the "wounds of time" are appreciated in the Wabi-sabi. On the other hand, if you decide to buy new home accessories, we recommend choosing sustainable, high-quality, handmade, or vintage products and materials.

Antique accessories and furnishing elements can be perfectly mixed with modern and minimalist furniture. This type of furniture combines the imperfections and asymmetries of furniture and accessories in an attractive and hospitable living space. Wabi-sabi points out that the home must be a comfortable space where one feels at ease. Pillows, for example, add comfort.

During the transformation, you can also decide to refresh the walls; look for inspiration in nature for the choice of colors. This will allow for a wide selection of colors, from soft pink or beige to soothing blue or green. Or, with decorative techniques, you can give the appearance of rusty iron or oxidized copper, obtaining different degrees of rust or oxidation.

Nothing is definitive. All things have a predefined course; they are born, live, and die. This inevitable circle of life forms a vital cornerstone in Japanese aesthetic philosophy.

Not surprisingly, in traditional Japanese architecture, since no building was to last too long, the constructions were made of wood, which has a natural time limit.

Unlike Western architecture, which is primarily made of concrete and carries the illusion of eternity, Japanese temples and houses have been rebuilt many times, even altering the original design.

Translated into a more homely environment, the Wabi-Sabi style means avoiding the shiny, the perfect, and the uniform for an attitude more exposed to use, time, and the elements, and therefore unique.

Remember that there is always ethics behind aesthetics, which generates a feeling of calm, evoked by elements such as light furniture and organic shapes.

Recovery is an integral part of the design. This translates into fewer "catalog" furniture choices to prefer objects assembled, found, repaired, and relocated in the same environment.

Time becomes art. Light is the protagonist, even when it is dark or chiaroscuro. Antique furniture or poor art emerges from nowhere to reinforce the forms of architecture.

Wabi-sabi is the perfect antidote to the rampant pompous, cloying and institutional beauty style that was and is desensitizing Western society.

The choice of materials is an elegant chromatic path that leads from white to black through neutral and natural tones, where the presence of the others enhances the identity of each color. It is a tactile and material exploration: from smooth surfaces like silk to irregular and imperfect ones with natural grain.

The wabi-sabi style "lives" of beauty, that of every day.

As you may have understood, the materials flee from millimeter perfection:

- Gypsum and hand-brushed plaster.

- Rough or inlaid parquet.

- Oxidized metals.

- Pieces of recovered marble form a "background" made of sculptural elements.

Time becomes a place: without a glossy finish.

The wabi-sabi style is not for everyone, and it is useless to delude oneself. It is a design attitude that starts from a place and a specific state of mind.

The wabi-sabi style is not decorative. It left no room for the factory's wallpapers, glass, and mirrors yesterday. It cannot be done for just one room because the others have already been furnished.

Instead, this style:

- Dress the space with charm and suggestion

- It prefers soft textures to the touch and of high aesthetic quality.

- It mixes rusty metals, gold foil, exposed concrete, and textured paints

- Use aged wood, not Ikea lacquers

- Use opaque fabrics and materials, not the glass and chrome steel

- He is not afraid to recover objects and furnishings, even if they are broken or in bad condition

• Use rough concrete

• It does not use stadium spotlights, psychedelic lights, or exaggerated LED cuts.

• Natural light becomes the undisputed protagonist, and the furniture seems to be chosen and arranged perhaps more as a pretext to enhance it.

• Prefers soft fabrics in natural materials (cotton, jute, linen, wool...)

• It does not repaint or clean up after a while, years. Cracks and the patina of time are examined and treated if necessary.

• It generates sophisticated and not at all trivial spaces, albeit minimal.

• In practice, some materials can be used or preferred over others.

CHAPTER 10

JAPANDI, THE STYLE THAT MARRIES HYGGE AND WABI-SABI

Japandi, a word that combines the terms Japan and Scandinavian, indicates a furnishing style that harmoniously blends the characteristics of the hygge and wabi-sabi philosophies.

For several years now, the Scandinavian style has been characterized by warm and welcoming environments where nature plays an important role. Scandinavian furniture features simple lines, natural materials, and great functionality. The philosophy that animates the contemporary Scandinavian style was born in Denmark and is called Hygge.

Japanese furniture represents the essence of minimalism, elegance, and sobriety. The search for aesthetic purity gives life to virtual environments characterized by rigorous lines. Perhaps to balance such rigor, the wabi-sabi philosophy, which seeks beauty in imperfection, introduces handcrafted objects, preferably handmade and described by some defects.

Despite the geographical distance, these two styles have two points in common: minimalism and the use of natural materials. The Japandi style grafted onto these two peculiarities a sober and elegant character, typical of Japanese aesthetics, combined with extreme functionality of Scandinavian origin. Today, the Japandi type is increasingly sought after, but this is not new. It was created over 150 years ago.

The harmonious Japanese style arose from long-standing cultural ties between Japan and Denmark. The unique types of the two countries began to interact more than 150 years ago when Danish architects, artists, and designers traveled to Japan in search of new inspiration. They were one of the first people in the West to come to the country across newly opened borders, as they had been closed for the previous 220 years.

However, the admiration is mutual. The Danish style has been sought after for decades in all corners of Japan. Both types are characterized by respect for artisans, handmade products, natural materials, and a positive approach to simplicity. You will also find similarities in the complete functionality of space and a balanced vision of life.

The colors of the Japandi style are sober and contemplate a palette ranging from neutrals to pastel shades. White, gray, and different shades of light brown can be used without moderation. For accents, green, blue, or yellow, but strictly in pastel shades. Gold to be dosed with caution but essential, perhaps included in complements and accessories.

After all, the notes of color are dictated by the materials used, mostly natural. Wood is the absolute protagonist, both painted and raw, to be chosen in the bamboo, lime, or oak varieties. Metal, fabrics such as linen or cotton, ceramic, stone, and paper are the other materials to be preferred.

Furnishing in the Japandi style means coming to terms with oneself, putting aside the tendency to accumulate objects or fill the rooms with furniture. Provide built-in wardrobes and closets to store the inevitable ballast of unnecessary items unless you are already an expert in decluttering. The Japandi environments are characterized by minimal furniture and a few complimentary objects.

For the essential comfort corner, you can abound with cushions, blankets, and rugs to mix natural fabrics such as wool, linen, cotton, or vegetable fibers.

The importance of lighting and greenery

Lighting and greenery play a vital role in Japandi furnishings. Austerity and minimalism must be dampened on pain of a cold and unwelcoming environment. Warm and differentiated lighting, which manages to create exciting chiaroscuro in the background, can be obtained with different lighting devices.

Suspension lamps are placed on tables and kitchen islands, alternating with countertop lamps for the most intimate corners. For general lighting, choose floor lamps with a discreet design, bearing in mind that the light must always be muted.

Do not skimp on the green to complete the picture: succulents, green indoor plants, and elegant orchids will enliven the environment. Use earthenware pots and handcrafted ceramic pot holders or glass jars to insert twigs, leaves, and bamboo canes.

Combining two very distant styles can offer the opportunity to bring out character and personality.

A hybrid style like the Japandi one guarantees a balance between Japanese elegance and Scandinavian essential modernity.

The meeting point between these styles is represented by simplicity together with certain aesthetic minimalism, for which clean, tidy, and essential environments are recreated while maintaining their functionality.

The colors used by the Japanese and Scandinavian styles differ significantly since the first is based on earthy nuances, while the second mainly uses white.

Japandi style perfectly mixes these color palettes, playing with the contrasts between bright colors and natural colors to create exciting and relaxing environments from an aesthetic point of view.

Japandi -style space, we could put dark accents in a light setting, such as charcoal or dark brown objects.

Or, vice versa, insert lighter furnishings reminiscent of the Scandinavian style, in a dark space, with sage green or gray tones.

These additions can be made thanks to pillows, rugs, and frames; however, remembering not to overdo it to keep a minimalist look.

The role of natural elements

For a Japandi -style interior, one of the essential characteristics is the presence of natural elements, another point in common between the Scandinavian and Japanese styles.

The addition of plants gives the rooms an atmosphere of well-being and tranquility, provided by the shades of green.

The strong Japanese influence in the Japandi style, however, wants the quality of the plants to be given more importance than quantity.

Consequently, selecting a few specimens with distinctive and elegant leaves will be ideal.

The functional furnishings

The furnishings in the Japandi style have essential and clean lines, keeping functionality as a priority aspect.

To create a perfect fusion, it will be necessary to blend light-toned Scandinavian furniture with soft lines and dark and elegant furniture typical of Japanese interiors.

It is a combination capable of balancing rigor and sinuosity, typical of the Japandi style.

The Japanese furniture based on traditional culture is characterized by the low table, which gives the possibility to stay as close as possible to the earth.

To mix styles, you could opt for beds, coffee tables, and low benches, taking care to leave ample free space.

Furnishing accessories and materials

As for furniture, functionality and quality are more important than quantity for accessories and furnishing accessories.

The Scandinavian style focuses on a few pieces which give well-being and are welcoming, such as rugs and soft cushions, while the Japanese style focuses on authenticity.

A perfect fusion knows how to choose functional, simple, and essential accessories.

Think, for example, of adding wooden Venetian blinds, which are beautiful and essential to look at aesthetically and, at the same time, capable of guaranteeing privacy and energy saving.

The materials must be natural and preferably of craftsmanship.

Craftsmanship is one of the most authentic expressions of this thought since the objects are not made perfect in series, but each one is created with its characteristic imperfection.

The selection must include simple and quality materials, such as linen, cork, terracotta, and jute.

All with the typical feature of giving the rooms a welcoming and comfortable atmosphere.

Eliminate the superfluous

The Japandi is the fusion of two interior design styles, based on the concept of essentiality, created by eliminating the superfluous in favor of the functional.

The mix must give life to airy, tidy, bright, and clean environments, capable of having everything you need to be condensed into a few elements.

In short, this style goes perfectly with the need for decluttering at home, making it more essential, clean, and welcoming.

CHAPTER 11

THE KITCHEN IN JAPANDI STYLE

In this chapter, we report tips on creating a Japanese kitchen. This style best suits those who want to approach wabi-sabi design but perhaps do not currently have the psychological or economic force to transform their kitchen. So if you're going to close wabi-sabi one step at a time, this is the easiest way.

Japandi style kitchen is minimal and essential, characterized by furniture with clean and square lines, a few colors, and furnishing elements are chosen with great care and care, in a not unexpected way.

Japandi style of furniture was born as a hybrid style. It contains the best of typically oriental aesthetics - especially Japanese - and the characteristic features of the Nordic Scandinavian style.

Precisely what they are looking for in the Japandi style of furniture. According to the Japandi aesthetic, everything has its function, and, not secondarily, nothing is ever out of place. In an often chaotic home environment such as the kitchen, the Japandi style of furniture is an actual injection of rigor and minimalism.

Japandi style kitchen

Since Japandi is a hybrid style, the reference color palette contains shades dear to both kinds from which it originates. In the kitchen, soft and light shades find ample space, starting from white to the entire range of beiges.

Like in the Scandinavian style, these soft shades - by the way, effortless to combine - are a must when furnishing the kitchen in Japandi style.

Even if there is no lack of darker and more intense touches of color, dark browns and blacks, typical of the Japanese décor style, is equally popular with the Japandi. Depending on your preferences, you can decorate the kitchen with lighter or darker shades.

The ideal is to wisely combine them, creating a beautiful harmony as a whole.

Wood and other materials for Japandi furniture in the kitchen

Japandi-style kitchen. Just as the Japanese oriental tradition suggests, it is wood that dominates. Therefore, the wooden kitchen is the closest to the Japandi style, in which other natural materials also find space.

Bamboo, rattan, and rice paper evoke a strong bond with nature. Just think of the hood or the seats for some accessories or single functional kitchen elements; for example, steel and cast iron are also recommended.

Chairs, tables, and inevitable furnishing accessories

The Japanese-style kitchen is usually characterized by low furniture, and there are those who, by furnishing their home in the Japandi style, follow this rule. Depending on your preferences, insert furniture elements such as more or more miniature low chairs and tables. As for the chairs, there are many options to choose from.

Wooden stools when combined with a peninsula. Alternatively, opt for rattan armchairs with a comfortable and enveloping seat.

As already mentioned, the Japandi style strongly believes in rigor and order. Therefore, there is no lack of cabinets full of doors (preferably sliding) to keep the environment as tidy and "clean" as possible in a perfect Scandinavian Japanese kitchen.

As far as lighting is concerned, the ideal is pendant lamps, with a contemporary and very trendy appeal. Choose them in bamboo or wicker according to the Japanese aesthetic.

The importance of plants in the kitchen according to the Japandi style

Anyone who knows the Japandi style knows that plants play a fundamental role in furnishing the house. These symbolize the bond with nature and with the earth. Place a more or less large plant on the table or the kitchen cabinet, preferring the green and luxuriant ones. Even bonsai is confirmed as an excellent choice.

Alternatively, decorate the room with many cherries or orange blossom branches to dry and store in a vase.

CHAPTER 12
IDEAS FOR CREATING A WABI-SABI
LOW STYLE KITCHEN COST

If you do not intend to spend too much and therefore not make too invasive interventions, you can start from the walls, for example, with an oriental wallpaper.

If you don't want to ruin the entire original wall, some stencils recall the Japanese style, depicting peach blossoms, bamboo canes, oriental writings, etc.

Suppose your kitchen is "far" from Japan. In that case, you could cover the furniture, choosing on the internet or in any DIY store models of adhesive paper that, for example, replicates wood, the material of choice for the Japanese.

You can also focus on chandeliers, especially if your kitchen is made up of a peninsula, on which to drop classic Japanese lanterns, in rice paper or fabric... even on a wooden table.

Another touch of style can be given with wooden utensils insight, such as spoons and ladles, or even by hanging Japanese ceramic plates... all simple ideas to make but above all inexpensive.

Challenging and luxurious solutions

The possibility of wanting to renovate the kitchen entirely and the various accessories and furnishing accessories of your Open Space cannot be excluded.

You will certainly start from the kitchen... opt for a simple material: wood and for linear and square shapes.

It will be up to you to opt for the peninsula, table, or both... wooden stools with wicker seats and wooden chairs to combine oriental cushions.

If you have much space in your house, you can find a corner to place that tea service directly from Kyoto, perhaps under a shelf on which you will add your favorite teas and herbal teas.

And those Japanese ceramic bowls, where do you usually serve ramen to your friends on cold winter evenings?

Insert a showcase between the kitchen cabinets; you can store them in plain sight and indoors, so they won't collect dust!

To illuminate by creating an effect of lights and shadows, which are very zen, you can imagine the light that penetrates between one intersection and the other of the bamboo... these chandeliers will float on your table, softening the squares of the surrounding furniture.

Japanese style tableware

A kitchen with a Japanese design cannot fail to be treated in detail, so if you want, you can exaggerate, starting with cutlery, for example.

The time has come to abandon the belief that the Japanese eat only with chopsticks; they use cutlery just like us, different in colors, materials, and shapes but still cutlery!

In Japan, ceramic is used a lot; the difference lies in how it is decorated, the colors, and the elements depicted on the dishes, such as flowers, samurai, geometric figures, and Japanese calligraphic writings.

Of course, wooden dishes are also widely used.

Japanese style dishes

Flat plates for sushi and funds for the food of choice, which in Japan is rice, ramen, and broths based on meat and vegetables, and bowls for sauces that almost always accompany their typical dishes.

Japanese style centerpieces and tablecloths

Greenlight also to grandmother's doilies, doilies, and embroideries that you can use on your kitchen furniture and the table under glasses.

Finally, you can set your table with that hand-painted tablecloth you have kept in the kit until today to make a great impression on your guests.

Otherwise, you can choose Japanese-style tablecloths and napkins, in pure cotton or linen, or for quick meals, some wicker placemats to unroll at the moment and go... more luxurious than that!

Japanese style decor

Finally, we think of further embellishing the environment created so far with plants and flowers. You can think of a bonsai, a succulent plant, as a centerpiece.

Think of orchids if you love flowers with a delicate and exquisite appearance.

Peach blossoms are the must-have of Asian countries like Japan, but it's also true that they are seasonal flowers, so they don't last all year round.

The alternative is that of fake flowers; in this way, they will last and require no care, if not a dusting.

Open space ideas

You can create a living room with fabric sofas, carpets, strictly low tables, poufs, and wicker baskets if the room is enormous.

Imagine a large painting on the sofa wall that perhaps depicts a buddha," the great wave" of Hokusai, samurai, flowers, or a simple Zen landscape.

Tall and narrow glass vases are also preferred. Fill the bottom with stones and stick some bamboo inside them; the effect will be 100% Japanese.

CHAPTER 13

HOW TO FURNISH THE BEDROOM

W ood is, therefore, the material you cannot give up if you want to furnish the bedroom.

This material becomes the basis for the floor, but also the furniture. Lightwood and even raw wood should be preferred.

The actual unique and particular combination is the combination of wood with vibrant materials, such as dark marble, which is also used to create elegant Japanese-inspired coatings.

Another material is paper. Rice paper is used for making lamps or light paintings. He also uses bamboo for the decorations of the environment and rich fabrics that have simple, linear, or solid-colored patterns and embellishments.

The decorations suit this style for your bedroom, trend towards sobriety and elegance. In particular, plants play a leading role; large indoor plants make the environment lively and cheerful.

Secondly, wallpapers are of great importance. Scenographic designs, inspired by pure geometric shapes and Japanese art, are made of natural subjects, leaves, and colors such as gold, black and deep green.

Another element that you cannot give up for the bedroom is the cabinets, bedside tables, or benches with simple lines. In particular, use furniture that prioritizes empty spaces over full ones. Everything becomes light and becomes minimal.

As for the secondary decorations, use a framed mirror and paintings, which reproduce within them simple subjects or drawings inspired by lineart, the art of depicting six subjects, people, or passages using a continuous black line on a white background.

When referring to Japan, a technologically advanced nation immediately comes to mind, at the forefront of most sectors, full of skyscrapers and full of luxury and comfort. These are certain truths that sometimes cannot entirely refer to the style of Japanese houses.

Minimalist and aseptic at first glance, Japanese homes are straightforward and economically furnished, as the inhabitants of this nation prefer order and simplicity. Despite this, mainly because they are very different from ours, Japanese houses are full of character, which is why we love so much to be inspired in design by this Eastern culture.

The Japanese bed stands out from all the others for its shallow height, able to raise even the lowest ceilings. You can either buy cheap or create a bed of this size using thin wooden planks. An oriental-style alternative to the standard bed is the futon, a type of bed that can be rolled up in the evening and rolled out in the morning, which allows the bedroom to be converted into any other room for everyday use. On the leading e-commerce sites, it is also available at 70 euros.

The lights

The lights can increase the oriental atmosphere inside the Japanese bedroom. Usually, the classic Japanese lamps are used, with small dimensions for the bedside tables and high ones to act as floor lamps. The style in question loves square and regular lines, so rectangular and square lights are perfect to be placed inside the bedroom. The small Japanese lamps, mostly made of bamboo, are available on the market for around 20 euros; the floor lamps, on the other hand, start at 40 euros.

Colors

The Japanese style is not very demanding for colors, but the most used are warm tones such as yellow, red, orange, and brown: the latter is also due to the presence of natural wood, a material widely used in this type of design. Among the cold colors, gray, black, and light blue win, as long as it is pastel or very soft.

Plants

Although Tokyo represents the typical metropolis with a western flavor, the Japanese are true to nature lovers. For this reason, they love to furnish their bedroom by inserting some plants, as long as they do not make the air suffocating. There are aloe vera, pothos, peace lily, and lavender among the perfect plants in the bedroom.

Doors and screens

Thinking about a Japanese home, one cannot help but imagine the classic sliding doors. Suppose it is impossible to convert the western doors into Japanese-style ones because the cost can even exceed 1000 euros. You can easily opt to introduce some wooden grids to the walls to give the bedroom that good quality. Squared and geometric effects that would be missing. The slats that make up the grid can be easily recycled from an old bed base.

Japanese screens

Another way in full Japanese style to divide the house's rooms is to insert screens of various sizes. There are all shapes, types, and colors, usually available at an affordable starting price of 30 euros: the screens most appreciated by the Japanese are the simple ones in shades of white or those with floral and fauna textures.

Even in the Western world, the charm of Japanese bedrooms is becoming more and more popular. These are simple yet visually striking and suggest a vast impression of serenity and balance. Japanese furniture today can present itself in various forms, from the hi-tech version to the one that combines the Japanese imprint with the Scandinavian one. The solutions are different, but one of the most popular in any case is the classic one, with fusuma, Tatami, futon, and so on.

Bedrooms need to be functional and elegant, and one inspired by the Land of the Rising Sun fulfills all these characteristics. Some essential accessories are required, such as a Japanese-style bed, a low nightstand, and other elements that we will discuss shortly.

The futon: the futon occupies a special place in Japanese bedrooms. We refer to the traditional flexible mattress, which can be placed directly on the floor or a low wooden bed. Due to its structure, the futon can be rolled up easily and stored in a wardrobe or large drawer in the morning. This allows you to save space and have a completely free and uncluttered floor. For this reason, the futon is also often used in guest rooms: it can be stored without problems and moves easily from one room to another.

In addition, the futon is "green" for the materials with which it is made! The best futons have cotton or wool padding: you can buy both types to alternate between summer and winter. The surface is soft but still able to offer the proper support to the spine. There are also latex futons and futons with coconut slabs to accommodate all needs. As for the coating, it can be either in cotton or zinc oxide. The result is eco-friendly, comfortable, and safe. The futon is a must for Japanese-style bedrooms. And maintenance is simple, as you need to avoid moisture.

The low wooden bed: those who do not want to place the futon on the floor could choose a soft wooden bed to match the traditional Japanese mattress. However, these accessories are perfect not only with futons but also with western latex or memory mattresses. Foam. The most suitable beds, in this context, are the interlocking ones: entirely made of wood, without metal details such as screws and nails. The wooden panels fit together, guaranteeing solidity and stability. A wooden bed is eco-sustainable, spectacular, and very comfortable. Wood is one of the fundamental materials in Japanese furniture, suggestive of its grain, natural, and capable of transmitting warmth and harmony.

The doors: fusuma and shoji - When you need to set up a room, it is essential to take care of the choice of doors. The Japanese ones are called fusuma and shoji. An internal door, which connects the bedroom to the house's other rooms, is called fusuma. It is rectangular panels with a wooden core and a cover of fabric, cardboard, or rice paper. The sliding takes place on wooden tracks. Instead, the term shoji is used for exterior doors. These elements are made of wood and paper and are truly beautiful.

The Tatami - In Japanese bedrooms, you could also arrange a tatami: the classic mat for the floor, in a rush, and rice straw with fabric edges. The Tatami can be of various heights, ranging from those typical of Japan (5-6 cm) to those lowered, more similar to Western solutions, of 2.5 cm. Foldable, rollable, rubber tatamis, and so on. The possibilities are endless, as are the decorative motifs!

Furniture and Accessories: to conclude, what else is missing in a Japanese-style bedroom? A low wooden bedside table, just like the bed, or even a tatami bedside table with a rice straw interior is lovely. To keep personal effects, you need to assemble a wooden wardrobe with a pure and minimal design and some wooden shelves. As for accessories, lamps of wood and rice paper are evergreen. A themed print of a Japanese artist to hang on the wall, and that's it!

CHAPTER 14

THE BATHROOM

The best bathroom color in this style is neutral.

In terms of color, most colors are pretty neutral. Warmer and more earthy colors are ideal; they will calm your mind and create a friendly atmosphere. So choose, for example, beige, cream or brown. To liven up the interior, you will consider the contrast of dark colors - emerald, indigo, or dark purple. But you don't have to overdo them! As for patterns, it's best to avoid them.

Furniture and love for wood

Japandi style prefers low-to-the-ground furniture. This custom promotes people's connection with the earth and their sensory perception of nature. So are, for example, the cabinets under the sink, which also save space. The furniture lines are clean and minimalist. And what material to choose? Definitely wood. One option is to buy furniture that mimics a wooden surface, but you can also look for natural wood. In this case, tropical woody plants used to humidity are ideal. However, expect a higher price.

The furniture must be chosen carefully because it is a distinctive and bold element. Don't forget the quality: always buy only from certified producers. One option is to use recycled older pieces.

Faucet for sink and basin

Another essential element is, of course, the sink. In the bathroom, it will stand out both freely placed on a support surface and classically connected directly to the washbasin cabinet. To emphasize the harmonious atmosphere in the room, you will choose round shapes: both round and oval washbasins are made.

Also, don't forget the basin mixer. It should match the sink, so if possible, choose products from the same series of products from similar lines. Since the Japanese style prefers simplicity to complex shapes, choose between lever taps rather than knob taps. However, you can also select a contactless tap: it is not just very modern but also highly hygienic.

Bath or shower?

In every bathroom, whatever the style, there is an element that will attract our attention at first glance. Most often, it is a bath or shower. The Japanese-style bathroom does not prefer any of the options. It is up to you which option to choose. If the room is spacious, we recommend choosing a freestanding bathtub: it will look truly unique. It compares all the different designs for the shower and chooses the best one. Here too, however, the more the rounder, the better.

Walk-in showers are also an exquisite solution. However, you can also choose a custom-made atypical shower, which everyone will admire in your bathroom. The same goes for the bathtub; in no case can there be limits to your imagination.

Minimal accessories

Don't go overboard in the Japanese bathroom with accessories. In this style, functionality comes first. The decoration will be minimal: it mainly consists of plants, glass products, and handmade ceramics.

urushi wallpapers, shibori fabrics, bonsai, or paper lamps. Even the walls should not be too decorated; we recommend choosing a dominant decoration and adding only a few details. One such dominant feature may be, for example, a frameless mirror, which optically enlarges and illuminates the space. Last but not least, you can use fabrics made from natural materials for decoration.

CHAPTER 15

THE LIVING ROOM

Create a magnificent living room using the Japanese style philosophy. Recreate the Rising Sun atmosphere in the living room by studying furniture arrangements and aiming for a Zen and minimal lifestyle.

Escaping the allure of the Far East appears difficult for some people: once upon a time, it was said that Africa was sick, but today, it seems that Japan piques the interest of many who usually travel to the Rising Sun in search of a modern destination with an exotic flavor. To be inspired and meditate, as prescribed by ancient Zen philosophies.

When you return from your vacation, you should re-propose the series of furnishings that define the authentic Japanese style in your apartment.

Let's try to design a modern living room but, at the same time, is strongly influenced by Japanese culture and its millenary history.

Let's consider the essential points of this style before opening your wallet and wandering around shopping malls and ethnic shops specializing in the furnishings that offer this style.

The dominant philosophy in Japanese homes is based on the search for harmony and lightness, which are essential founding points of the Zen lifestyle.

The apartment, and thus its rooms, are designed and studied so that its coexistence and stay inside the theme is marked by the essential, to the point where it can be identified, in some features, as similar to the minimalist style.

As a result of the success of sliding doors allows you to join rooms with a simple gesture while also allowing light and airflow between spaces to flow freely.

Colors reflect this spirit of life, always harmonious and soft; thus, the prohibition of temptations to overdo it with flashy and contrasting chromatic games.

It is the triumph of different natural materials such as wood, mainly bamboo, which is used to make most of the furniture, and rice paper, which is used to cover the doors of wardrobes, sliding doors, and dividers.

The central station, the sofa, is placed against the wall to keep the passage as straightforward as possible: the table in front will be helpful for lunch or dinner. At the same time, you can sit on the cushions without collapsing or making large movements on the floor.

The Tatami, the carpet used for judo and karate competitions, is the most common surface coating in Japanese homes.

The Tatami is constructed with a wood or other material frame and then covered with woven and pressed straw to provide some resistance to body weight.

The sofa is crucial in the living room, especially in Japanese homes where rest and meditation are an essential part of daily life.

For those who appreciate tradition, the sofa has a distinctive wooden structure and a futon mattress, which can be placed on the floor for afternoon or night rest if you have visitors.

Let us recall that the futon is a comfortable roll-up mattress that is beaten in the morning to allow it to absorb air and be free of dust. Then it was wrapped like a sleeping bag.

The furnishings of traditional Japanese houses are sparse. The Zen philosophy imprints a lifestyle on minimalism; the search for essentiality and, therefore, tinsel and not very functional furniture are not foreseen.

Rectangular or square in shape, entirely in wood, it has accentuated edges while the colors remain on the classic brown of the wood or, in a more modern version, black.

They are used to discreetly divide rooms or create a corner within an environment, as is the case in the bedroom.

They must be easily moved and provide an interesting decorative element.

When you want to decorate in a meaningful way, images of landscapes, volcanoes, and country towns are often drawn on the shutters rather than gardens.

The dividers generally have a height of about 180 cm and have at least 3/4 doors.

Japanese style living room: lighting on the other hand, ceiling chandeliers have a distinct charm, with luminaires that have a simple shape, such as square, rectangular, or spherical, with regular dimensions.

The lampshades have no ornaments or designs, and the colors are dull and monotonous, primarily white, beige, or grey.

CHAPTER 16

THE FENG SHUI

Design rules, materials, and colors to furnish the house with the Feng Shui method for an apartment inspired by the teachings of Taoist philosophy.

How to design a Feng Shui furniture for the home? Before moving on to practical advice, it is good to know that the expression "Feng Shui" comes from Chinese and means "wind and water." It is an oriental discipline that combines practices of reading and interpreting buildings' landscapes, forms, and interior spaces to establish a perfect harmony between people and the environment.

According to this discipline, born about five thousand years ago, the arrangement of rooms and furnishings inside a house affects the energy inside and, consequently, the people who live there. Therefore, the goal of Feng Shui is to create a positive flow of energy in every room of the house through the creation of sober, comfortable, and tidy spaces.

Feng shui in Chinese means "wind and water." The wind is the sky, the air that carries the clouds swollen with rain, the water without which every creature on the planet could not survive. The ancient discipline of feng shui is considered indispensable and is a set of practices of reading and interpreting the landscape, the shapes of the buildings, and the spaces inside the buildings to avoid the negative influences of various kinds that can affect the structures the man.

The practice of feng shui is a five-thousand-year-old Chinese and Tibetan tradition with a Japanese equivalent in Ka-so. Ti-Li, or "blackbird art," symbolized the solar spirit, the god of geography and astronomy, whose teachings served as the foundation for agricultural and land planning practices

in ancient times.

This tradition is still very rooted in China and Hong Kong, so the first expert to be consulted is a Feng master when buying land or a building. Shui; his opinion affects the real estate market. Even when an economic activity suffers setbacks, it is customary to ask him for a response to any hostile energies set in motion by the type of architecture or interior decoration.

The aesthetic concepts of "beauty" and "harmony of proportions" and the economic ones linked to the exploitation of the territory and its characteristics are closely related to the practice of geomancy, that is, respect for subtle balances (earth, telluric, and energy of the sky, cosmic) to make the energies of the place favorable to human settlements.

According to this ancient Chinese discipline, the house-man relationship identifies the vibratory aspect of energy structures in

76

which subtle energy fields are identifiable, recognized as constituting a pattern within which a vital energy flows connected to all forms of life.

FENG SHUI: GENERAL RULES FOR FURNISHING

Feng Shui conceives the domestic space as a container that adapts to our personality and activities.

Below we propose some basic rules of organization of spaces and style for a perfect Feng Shui home.

Feng Shui at home: the position of command

In Feng Shui furniture, it is appropriate to establish the command position in some house rooms. The command position is located at the opposite corner from the door. At this point, you must place a bed, a desk, or a sofa: the aim is to reduce one's vulnerability by assuming a dominant position to control and enhance one's energy flow.

Design spaces with the Bagua map

The practical principles of Feng Shui are expressed through the Bagua, a Chinese term that means "eight trigrams." The Bagua is a geomantic map that matches an aspect of life, such as work, health, and social relationships, to every room in the house.

A Bagua map is composed as follows:

Eight sections (Gua) correspond to the sides of the octagonal map, which represent family, marriage, children, social relationships, career, knowledge, health, and wealth;

every Gua has a number that corresponds to the eight cardinal points, which helps know the personal energy of the inhabitants of the house;

every Gua is followed by a trigram, each with a different combination of lines: the solid ones represent the masculine yang, while the broken ones represent the feminine yin ;

the eight different combinations of the trigrams represent the forces generated by the five natural elements: fire, earth, metal, water, and wood;

the central area is occupied by the symbol of Tai Chi (Ying Yang), representing the balance and harmony of all Gua and, therefore, personal well-being and health.

To use the Bagua map, it must be superimposed on the floor plan of the house by matching the center of the map with the center of the house; it is necessary to make the entry point coincide with the water Gua. To facilitate furnishing with the Feng Shui method, the octagonal pattern can be replaced with a square model divided into nine areas, each marked by the Gua, the characterizing natural element, and the primary color.

Choose colors in a balanced way.

The colors yellow, ocher, brown, apricot, and gold belong to the earth element. They are associated with the cardinal points of the south-west (social relations and marriage), the north-east (knowledge and self-realization), and the center (health). Yellow is associated with patience, control, and tolerance; others have a calming effect and stimulate concentration; a light apricot tint conveys warmth and coziness and is ideal for a bedroom.

Green color belongs to the wood element and is associated with the east (family) and south-east (wealth, prosperity, and abundance) cardinal points. In particular, green favors balance, harmony, and peace. The green decoration for the walls should be chosen only if there are few plants in the room to avoid generating redundancy in the environment.

We are renewing the house with colors: practical ideas for any environment.

In Feng Shui furniture, black, blue, and light Blue is associated with the north direction (career) and falls under the element of water. Black symbolizes work, power, and money and stimulates the imagination; Blue has a calming effect, makes a room with little natural light bright and welcoming, and is suitable for bathroom decor. On the other hand, Blue is ideal for small spaces, helps fight insomnia, and is perfect for furnishing a small bedroom.

White is rarely used in China because it is the color of mourning. It is perfect for illuminating and restoring a sense of order. However, it should be avoided in icy environments and in children's bedrooms. Gray and neutral shades convey balance and stability; they are ideal for the walls and furnishings of a home office or study corner. Both colors belong to the metal element and are associated with the cardinal points west (children and creative projects) and the north-west (friendship and support).

According to Chinese tradition, red is the luckiest color, a symbol of passion, joy, and growth: it is used with caution to avoid making the environment aggressive; it is suitable for a living area, even in furnishing elements. Orange infuses happiness and constructive energy: in less-lighted environments, it helps to create a relaxing atmosphere. Pink refreshes the rooms and makes them more welcoming in the lighter shades. These colors fall under the element of fire and are associated with the southern cardinal point (fame and reputation).

Feng Shui favors natural materials.

Wood, stone, metal, and fabrics are the most suitable materials for furniture inspired by the Feng Shui method. Wood is considered a living material with multipurpose characteristics and can be used for furniture, fixtures, and flooring in any house room.

The stone elements - shiny or porous, even in travertine or slate - must be inserted in a balanced and essential way.

Metals are also crucial in a home furnished according to the Feng Shui method, with different characteristics based on their composition. If the metal furniture elements are shiny and reflective, it is better to place them in environments intended for relaxation.

Finally, fabrics, especially natural ones such as linen, silk, cotton, and wool, must be used in a balanced way in the areas intended for rest since their interwoven composition slows down the flow of energy.

The importance of decluttering

Feng Shui furniture requires careful space optimization: get rid of different objects to make more space available.

The accumulation of unused or disordered objects would prevent the flow of positive energies. The rooms must be cleaned and tidy every day, eliminating unnecessary things, clothing, and furnishings using ecological methods.

FENG SHUI FURNITURE FOR THE LIVING ROOM

In the Feng Shui furniture style, the living room must have a square or rectangular floor plan. The key element around which the entire arrangement of the furnishings revolves is the sofa, which must have a linear and rounded shape, with a high back and armrests. Place it against a wall, possibly respecting the control position described above, i.e., in the opposite corner from the door.

According to the Feng Shui style, the room must be furnished with space-saving elements, rounded and harmonious shapes, and made with natural materials such as wood.

The living room is the environment of relationships and the fire element, so the best choice is to use red or its shades, always considering the geographical position concerning the Bagua map and, therefore, the corresponding colors. Red, in some cases, can be too energetic: the best solution is to include colors and materials belonging to each element to balance the energy.

Plants are full of positive energy and can help balance energy flows. It is better to choose plants with soft-shaped leaves and avoid those with a pointed shape.

FENG SHUI FURNITURE IN THE KITCHEN

In an ideal Feng Shui home, the kitchen is rectangular in plan, facing south, well lit, comfortable, and has extensive work surfaces.

The arrangement of the furniture must take into account the flows of energy and the symbols of nature: stove and oven (fire) must never be placed near the refrigerator and dishwasher (water), or at least they must be separated by cupboards or wooden shelves, element that represents the control over the destructive relationship between water and fire. Arrange them so that you do not have your back on those who enter to control the environment completely.

The colors to choose from are different; each can perform a specific function in the kitchen based on its exposure and the elements that compose it. Generally, it is advisable to take advantage of the lighter shades that reflect the light by focusing on colors such as green, yellow, white, and those of the earth, both for the furniture and for the walls and dividing panels.

Orange represents joy and vitality, stimulates the appetite, and has a regenerating effect on the nervous system; yellow is ideal for a dynamic area such as the kitchen as it has a warming and energizing function; green balances all the other colors recall the plant world and transmits calm; finally, the cleanliness of the white, with cream or butter shades, can also be used for the worktop, to be balanced with furnishings in darker tones to create light color contrasts.

Spice racks, utensils, cutting boards, pantries, and wooden containers also allow you to obtain positive energy. If the house does not consist of a dining room, the table and chairs in the kitchen are also preferred in wood, a symbol of prosperity and family union.

To circulate positive energies while respecting the cardinal points and free the negative ones from the environment where the cook transforms food using the five elements: water, wood, fire, earth, and metal.

FENG SHUI FURNITURE IN THE BEDROOM

On the other hand, if the bedroom is in the front, a mirror hanging in front of the door, behind the median line of the house, will "push" the room back.

The feng shui attaches a lot of importance to the bedroom's layout. The bed should be placed across, with the head facing east. The optimal location is in the corner diagonally opposite the entrance, in such a way that you never have heads or feet pointing directly towards the door to the room.

Inwood or upholstered fabric, the headboard must be placed against a wall to obtain a greater sense of support and protection.

Even the bed height must be chosen carefully: it must not be too low. In general, solutions with integrated containers should be avoided to allow energy to circulate even under it.

On the sides of the bed, it is possible to place bedside tables, preferably round in shape, so that the energy does not flow directly onto the person who sleeps, destabilizing the rest.

On the bedside tables, it is recommended to keep lampshades that give an oriental touch to the bedroom and allow you to create a relaxed atmosphere. Alternatively, you can use lamps with adjustable light intensity via switches, ideal for establishing the most suitable lighting level according to your needs.

In Shui style bedroom, the wisest decision is to use pastel colors or neutral shades.

Green and blue are the colors of nature, therefore very relaxing, associated with care and refreshment. Purple is a balanced color linked to prosperity and financial abundance with its lavender undertones.

Even so-called "skin colors" with shades ranging from pale white to brown are good options for a bedroom: ivory, Pink, beige, chocolate and bronze give the room a calm and friendly feel.

Colors

Green is the color of fresh plants and nature; it symbolizes growth and study.

Red represents animal life and learning; it is a good omen, especially in combination with black.

White is the color related to money and is used in public places to call good luck.

Black is related to rest and settling (of ideas).

The feng shui recommends not placing mirrors in the bedroom due to their ability to disturb the energy field. Covering the mirrors during the night improves the quality of sleep considerably.

FENG SHUI FURNITURE IN THE BATHROOM

The element that characterizes the bathroom is water, a symbol of life and purification. This element can also be reproduced in the furnishings through furniture with soft, twisted, and wavy shapes and colors such as blue and light Blue. Green and white are also suitable for decorating the bathroom with the Feng Shui method as they represent nature and purity, respectively.

To avoid energy dispersion, the bathroom must be balanced with the earth element through different materials, such as marble and quartz, which are excellent for the sink and other surfaces. Even the ceramic tiles, glass, and stone reinforce the reference to the earth and the terracotta, light yellow and delicate beige colors. The balancing of the elements can also be obtained with metals, particularly brass if the bathroom is facing south.

To add elegance and warmth, plants of tropical origin can be used, suitable for hot and humid environments. In particular, if it is lit enough by natural light, the best plants to choose from are aloe vera, begonia, orchid, fern, and bamboo.

The mirror has a reflective ability which makes it an energy amplifier. Since it is associated with the water element, the mirror must have characteristics that make the environment more harmonious: round in shape, essential, and positioned to reflect the wall but not the bathroom fixtures.

Office

To respect the feng shui in the office, the worktable should be placed at the most vital point of the room so that the back is protected and the gaze can be directed at the door and window. What is in front of the workstation is also extremely important as it increases the Qi and is a source of inspiration. Therefore desks with a position facing a wall should be avoided.

Feng shui and architecture.

Western and Eastern architecture have the same basic concept: achieving a balance. However, while Western architecture reaches it through symmetry, Eastern architecture goes it through dynamism: a yin is never the same as yang: they are always in changing relationships now one dominates the other, and the task is balancing these two forces.

The four celestial animals of feng shui

People called feng shui to choose the ideal place to erect the village in ancient times. For this reason, the presence of the four celestial or emblematic animals that we can define as the guardians of the four directions had to be recognized in the landscape: the dragon, the tiger, the tortoise, and the red phoenix.

The feng shui and water

Water is linked to abundance, wealth, money, and communication. Therefore, a watercourse that flows calmly near the house is considered favorable, preferably from east to west, or a small lake to the south, which can enhance its beneficial presence, reflecting the sunlight. Water must always be present in the rooms of the house.

CHAPTER 17

KA-SO, THE FENG SHUI MADE IN JAPAN

F eng Shui is the oriental art of furnishing according to the harmonic canons of human well-being. This particular discipline was born in China at a very distant time, and, recently, it has been observed that already in the Neolithic, the tombs were conceived following an exact layout and construction method.

This doctrine also has its roots in very remote times, and, in 1983, some scholars from the University of Illinois in Chicago translated ancient texts in which all the principles of Ka-So are kept.

BETWEEN SPACE AND TIME

The Ka-So aims to generate a total harmony of the subtle energies within the home. The fourth dimension, time, represents a fundamental variable. In the Ka-So, the time component translates into the period of the year or the season. Therefore the arrangement of the bed or futon within the housing unit acquires a different function also based on this factor.

Lao Tzu, a Chinese sage who lived in the sixth century BC and was considered one of the founding fathers of Taoism, argued that "the essence of the ship is the void within it." The Japanese art of living also took up this consideration. Design is imagined beyond the standard three dimensions and sublimation of time, also understood as space. For this reason, Japanese houses are furnished with the bare minimum, which translates into the use of futons, tatami mats, and a few other accessories.

THE INFLUENCES OF CHINESE CULTURE

Ka-So is the fruit of notions imported to Japan by an itinerant Buddhist monk in the last decades of the sixth century. From that moment, the planning of cities also began to follow pre-established schemes, and actual departments for the supervision of architectural projects were established. Kyoto itself (capital of Japan until 1868) was designed according to the principles of Ka-So.

CHAPTER 18

IKEBANA: THE FASCINATING JAPANESE ART OF ARRANGING CUT FLOWERS

To give a Wabisabi touch to your rooms, you can try Ikebana, an ancient Japanese art for creating cut flower vases.

Japan always offers magnificent artistic ideas, which are always modern and current, although born in ancient times. Ikebana's case indicates the ancient Japanese art of arranging cut flowers, branches, stems, and leaves harmoniously and elegantly. The name Ikebana derives from the union of the word Ike, which in Japanese means "alive," and Bana, which means "flower." Unlike the Western habit of filling a vase with more and more flowers, even of different types, Ikebana art aims at minimalism; a vase will hold a few flowers, the bare essentials to bring out the inner qualities of the flowers.

Given their meticulous artistry, Ikebana compositions can be defined as art installations in all respects.

How to make an Ikebana

These harmonious floral compositions can be formed by different types of flowers, starting from the orchid to hydrangeas, from chrysanthemums to gerberas, and from roses to bamboo branches. The main rule for creating an Ikebana composition is to use all elements of an organic nature, whether they are flowers, herbs, components, or leaves. Branches and flowers are thus arranged to create a triangle: the longest chapter called Shin, the most important one, is considered as the element that extends towards the sky, the shorter branch, the Hikae, symbolizes the earth, while the intermediate one, the Soe, represents the man. We need to balance Shin, Hikae, and Soe harmoniously without too complex elaborations.

Kenzan is the basis for Ikebana, a fundamental element for shaping the course of the composition as desired. Available in different diameters, this heavy support has metal spikes that will be used to pierce the stems of the cut flowers and keep them in an upright position.

Vase: the vase will allow you to create a balance between all the natural elements used. You can choose the vase as you like; some prefer low containers, others tall vases with a vertical trend. The decision will also vary based on the type of flowers selected. Floral arrangements created in flat containers are called Moribana, while those modeled on tall containers are called Nageire.

Scissors will be invaluable for cutting branches and flowers, removing excess parts, or reducing the size. There are no detailed specifications on the scissors; the idea is to use a model with a comfortable handle and made of resistant material to cut even large branches easily.

The courses that allow you to learn how to create your Ikebana are increasingly popular; in detail, they will focus on understanding how to properly cut flowers and branches, evaluate the correct positioning, and preserve living materials for a long time.

If you are fond of elegant flower arrangements, you love everything to do with minimalism, and feel a great attraction towards oriental culture; you will only be fascinated by this beautiful ancient art of arranging cut flowers.

When you find yourself in front of an ikebana composition, do you also feel a sensation between adoration and disorientation?

This Japanese art, so rich in history, exudes a charm that can be intimidating; yet, to practice some styles of Ikebana, you don't need to be an expert.

Like many traditional Japanese arts, Ikebana also asks to be 'listening' to oneself and nature. The composition that Jenny shows us is created according to the Nageire style, characterized by the spontaneity of execution, which emphasizes the natural beauty of the material used. It contrasts with the more artificial and complex techniques created.

The composition consists of three main branches, accompanied by various smaller branches.

Choose a tall and narrow vase and fill it with water; it will lend itself to the horizontal shape we will give. To keep the branches in the desired position, you can build flat forks with pieces of extensions fixed against the vase's edge, forming a cross.

Take the aucuba branches and the stems of the two hydrangeas and remove the leaves from the part that will go into the water. Too long stems and components should be cut diagonally to anchor them to the vase. The stems are always cut underwater to ensure fast absorption and avoid bubbles in the lymphatic channels of the branch.

Now insert the branches into the vase. The Shin branch defines the character and line of the composition. It is one and a half or two times the length of the vase. In the horizontal Nageire, this branch rests on an imaginary horizon. The Soe branch is half of Shin and must be placed on the opposite side; the Hikae addition is a third of Shin and should be positioned in the center, at the bottom.

Lastly, insert the flowers, in our case, two hydrangeas: we have chosen them to respect seasonality and 'zero km. You can spray branches, flowers, and leaves with a vaporizer, especially if it's hot.

CHAPTER 19
HOW TO COVER A FLOOR WITH TATAMI

In Japan, the tatami floor has spread to almost all homes thanks to its particular characteristics that allow it to be used in the same room for multiple purposes. In fact, during the day, it can serve as the ideal support for the typical Japanese coffee tables and the Japanese zaisu chairs, helpful in having lunch or consuming the typical tea ceremony. In the evening, the Tatami becomes a comfortable bed by simply spreading a Futon, the traditional Japanese mattress, on it. In both Japan and the West, the tatami floor is also used in all gyms where martial arts are practiced, such as Judo and Karate, because it reduces the risk of injury when falling.

What is Tatami: characteristics and composition

The term Tatami indicates the single rectangular or square carpet made of woven and pressed rice straw, and the traditional Japanese floor is composed of several mats placed side by side. Over time, these mats have also been increasingly sought after in the west to create an environmentally sustainable environment free of harmful substances as it consists only of natural elements.

The edges of the Tatami are squared with precision to avoid the presence of gaps when they are placed side by side to create the coverings. Thanks to this possibility of perfectly fitting them, it is unnecessary to use adhesives to fix them to the floor.

The advantages of tatami floors

The materials that make up the high-quality tatamis are entirely natural, making them ecological and perfectly biodegradable products. The woven straw surface gives off a pleasant scent and offers a sense of comfort that massages the sole when you walk on it. Therefore, walking barefoot, without shoes, or with the traditional Zori slippers that can certainly not be missing in an authentic Japanese home is recommended.

Like expanded cork and wood fiber, the natural and organic composition of the straw acts as an excellent thermal insulator. Furthermore, since the air molecules trapped in the straw weave of the tatami floor are insulated from the outside temperature, they can maintain a constant temperature. Precisely for this reason, the tatamis have the advantage of making the rooms cool in summer and warm in winter. In this way, they contribute to creating a healthy environment in the house, purifying the air and mitigating any humid climate in the rooms.

The tatami floors also offer an excellent degree of acoustic insulation, both thanks to the sound-absorbing properties of the straw that allows it to absorb a large part of the sound energy and because the thickness of the weave absorbs shocks and, therefore, noises.

When the individual tatami mats are put together to cover a floor, particular designs can be formed on the floor that strike for their perfect symmetry, creating scenic interlocking effects. Here are some examples of the compositions that can be made by combining tatamis of the same or different sizes:

Any interior floor can be covered with a bit of creativity, enhancing irregularities such as columns or walls with particular angles. Suppose the dimensions of the tatami panels do not match perfectly with the measurements of your room. In that case, you can also make custom-made tatami floors without cutting the carpets because they would almost certainly risk wearing out over time. These frames are usually colored black or wenge to make them uniform to the color of the edges of the tatamis. However, it is also possible to color them with other colors to match the rest of the other furnishings.

With wood, you can also create other additions to the tatami floor that enhance its design and offer practical solutions for the daily use of the environment.

For example, if you want the tatami floor to reach the house entrance, we can create a wooden island in front of the door that facilitates entry and allows you to take off your shoes without stepping on the Tatami as soon as possible enter the house. Or it is possible to create wooden frames that form islands in the middle of the floor, which can serve as a support for oriental vases such as our bamboo vases or suggestive Zen fountains.

Suppose you want to create a tatami floor in rooms where you also want to place furniture, such as a chest of drawers or wardrobes. In that case, you can make elevations of the same height as the carpets (about 6 cm) under the table to allow you to open the drawers or doors easily.

Finally, if you want to preserve an existing door that opens toward the tatami floor, you can cut the lower part of the door to align it with the new tatami floor, which will be about 6 cm higher than the previous floor.

Shoji sliding doors or walls are traditional Japanese room dividers made with a wooden frame on which rice paper is mounted. Japanese. Shoji sliding doors are particularly appreciated for the light and translucent consistency of washi rice paper, which filters the light and spreads it evenly throughout the room.

CHAPTER 20

HOW TO CREATE A TERRACE WITH A ZEN GARDEN

How do you furnish a Zen-style deck? What elements must not be missing? Find out how to design an outdoor space to find balance and harmony. Take a cue from these decor ideas to create a beautiful Zen terrace.

Balance and harmony are two basic principles of Zen art, a word that encompasses many oriental meditative disciplines aimed at achieving tranquility and greater self-awareness.

The style of furniture that reflects this philosophy of life is expressed through modern and essential-looking furniture, few colors and most natural, and the inevitable presence of the four natural elements: water, fire, earth, and air.

Designing a harmonious and peaceful space in your home is not difficult at all, but to create a place where you can relax or where you can meditate, we suggest you consider the idea of creating a Zen terrace.

Not sure where to start? Do not worry: here are furnishing ideas and practical advice to design a perfect outdoor space.

The project must reflect a pleasant and as natural place as possible, where the placement of each element responds to a specific need. Here is what should never be missing in the design of a Zen terrace:

- Minimal style furnishings: a Zen terrace is characterized by the presence of few but essential furnishings. Sofas, a low table, a meditation mat, and lots of comfortable cushions

- Prevalent of neutral and natural colors: beige, brown and black, white, blue, green, and yellow.

- Elements of nature: the presence of nature is essential to create an atmosphere of harmony and serenity. Therefore, plants, stones, and water from an electric fountain must not be missing, but also natural materials such as wood and rattan, flanked by furnishing accessories in sisal, hemp, and jute

- Asymmetries: nature is indomitable and chaotic, so the terrace must reflect this wild spirit through an asymmetrical arrangement of the various elements.

For the flooring, it would be preferable to opt for wooden platforms or interlocking modular tiles to be alternated with bands of stones or pebbles. Sand and gravel also give a decidedly natural look, but it would be better to reserve them for the green corners of your Zen terrace for convenience.

As for wood, you prefer teak, wengé, or wood with more amber shades such as Douglas: in addition to being hard and resistant, they give back a warm, natural and enveloping atmosphere. And walking or meditating barefoot will always be a pleasure.

When choosing furnishings, prioritize natural materials, such as wood or bamboo. Ecological materials are also perfect, such as rattan and poly-rattan, always preferred in light wood shades. The colors tend to be neutral and enlivened by some hints of brighter color and fabrics with optical or tropical prints.

As for the furniture design, I prefer modern low furniture, characterized by well-defined and essential lines. The minimal style is undoubtedly the most suitable trend for furnishing a Zen terrace.

Do not forget to insert a corner dedicated to meditation and tea: place a low table on a round carpet of woven rope and arrange large colored cushions or Japanese poufs in natural straw.

Lighting: how to create zen atmospheres

Lighting is an essential component of the Zen terrace because it recreates a harmonious and suggestive atmosphere from sunset to sunrise. Choose warm and natural lights, opting for lantern-shaped suspended lamps, to give that Japanese-style Zen touch that will immediately make the difference.

Place candles or candles of various sizes on the tables, placing them on a tray or in a glass bowl filled with water. Finally, don't forget to illuminate the plants and the darkest corners of your terrace by installing adjustable spotlights or a modern lighting system built into the floor.

We also offer you an equally suggestive decorative idea, namely the purchase of large outdoor vases with integrated LED: thanks to their soft light, your evenings on the terrace will immediately become more magical.

You can create a karesansui, a term for the Japanese Zen garden, if space permits. You will need to create a flat area enriched with gravel, pebbles, and stones of various sizes.

Alternatively, you can create a vertical one by installing masonry planters on the wall embellished with green leafy plants or the beautiful Japanese maple. On the terrace, it would be preferable to opt for the dwarf variant to avoid problems with space management.

Other plants that should never be missing are outdoor bonsai and bamboo plants. The latter should be placed in large rectangular planters so that their height can be exploited to create dividing spaces between one area of the terrace and another.

To give the last touch in Zen style, insert some decorative details of significant effect, remembering not to overdo it: essentiality is an essential factor, and too many decorations could make the environment anything but Zen!

CHAPTER 21
MISTAKES NOT TO BE MADE FOR A
WABI-SABI DESIGN

The wrong furniture, the incorrect arrangement of furniture and accessories, and even not choosing the right decorations are just some of the ten mistakes not to make when decorating your home in the wabi-sabi style. So let's see in detail what else we need to pay attention to.

Furnishing in this style is not easy. One must always look for harmony and an outstanding balance in the arrangement of every single object. Furthermore, it is a culture very distant from ours that reflects all its traditions in furnishing the house.

Because of this, it's easy to make mistakes. To help you better follow this trend, we have listed ten typical mistakes not to make.

1. Using too much furniture

Japanese style loves simplicity. Furthermore, a balance must be created in the environments. This means that the relationship between full and empty spaces must always be well balanced.

Considering that there is usually not a lot of square footage available, it would be a mistake to get caught up in the urge to buy too much furniture and fill each room more than necessary with unnecessary pieces of furniture.

2. Choose bulky furniture

If you want to furnish this style, you will have to give up the elaborate furniture full of decorations or inlays.

On the contrary, furniture made of wood or other natural materials with clean lines is preferred. Remember that Japanese houses are tiny, so the table must be as functional as possible.

3. Opt for the classic bed

Today there are many types of beds. We can choose between various materials and also different kinds of heights. So don't choose a classic bed in a home.

In this case, if you want to respect tradition, you have to opt for a futon. It is a mattress wrapped in comfortable blankets placed directly on the floor.

4. Place the chairs next to the table

When furnishing the kitchen or dining room, choosing a lovely large table and then adding matching chairs comes naturally.

However, if you are furnishing in Japanese style, this is a mistake not to make. The Japanese eat sitting on cushions on the floor so that you won't need chairs. As for the table, however, opt for shallow specific models.

5. Arrange the objects symmetrically

Don't arrange the objects symmetrically. Strange as this may seem, the Japanese do not like symmetry because it is compared to stillness.

Arranging the objects not all on the same line represents dynamism. This is good as it helps stimulate creativity.

6. Choose the wrong decorations

As much as the Japanese style loves simplicity, decorations in the home must not be missing anyway. However, we must evaluate which are the most suitable s and try not to overdo them.

Some porcelain may be on display, but nothing too modern. Flowers and candles are also welcome, as all objects contain water, such as small fountains that help you relax.

7. Forget about plants

Among the fundamental decorations when furnishing in Japanese style, we cannot fail to mention the plants, in particular, the bamboo and the bonsai.

They symbolize this culture and are considered real good luck charms. So forgetting them surely would be a mistake not to make.

8. Leave the walls bare

The walls of a house must constantly be embellished, certainly in the right way. Often, panels are placed as decoration, and there is no need to add anything else.

In other cases, however, paintings are welcome as long as they portray natural landscapes, flowers such as cherry trees, or are the typical Japanese prints.

9. Don't design large windows

Japanese culture pays excellent attention to the inside and the outside balance. This is reflected in a continuity also between the inside and the outside of the house.

For this, large windows overlooking the garden are essential. Avoid putting up curtains or anything else that could block your view.

10. Don't do decluttering

We have said that according to the wabi-sabi, one must accept imperfection. So you can leave the house a bit 'in diosrdine, but remember that you must always try to eliminate the extra.

CHAPTER 22
THE DECLUTTERING

Tabi-sabi philosophy, there is no place for the extra. Everything must be functional. Without forgetting that the extreme mental disorder, accumulating things in bulk in a maniacal way limits the spaces inside the house and our minds. So let's see how we can free up the areas outside and inside us.

The KonMari method by Marie Kondo: what it is and where to start

We have already talked about decluttering in the past, but making room in the house also has another famous name! You have often heard about it: the KonMari method, invented by cleaning guru Marie Kondo, has conquered the world.

A bestseller that has only anticipated a real revolution in tidying, or rather the Netflix series "Let's tidy up with Marie Kondo. " Boom.

However, a method promises to restore order, light, and joy in the home (and perhaps in life) through many small tricks applied rigorously.

All very interesting, but in practice… where do you start?

According to the KonMari method, it is not necessary to proceed by room, but by category of objects, strictly in this order: clothes, books, papers, and Komono (or... miscellany).

Everything, therefore, belongs to a macro or sub-category. It is strongly recommended to collect all the objects belonging to the same category and arrange them on the floor - or in any case, on a flat surface, which can be a bed or a table - and analyze them one by one., choosing their fate.

Before deciding what to keep and throw away, and before letting yourself go of the memories, ask yourself: "Does it make me happy?"

We must surround ourselves with beautiful things which remind us of happy moments and which, looking at them, make us feel joy and well-being.

So let's throw away that pair of jeans that we've been promising ourselves to wear for two years when we have lost 5 kg (making us feel inadequate in the meantime), away with those books that collect dust and haven't opened for ten years, out with that box full of notes, ribbons, pens, and objects of various kinds that have been closed for months.

Not everything should be thrown in the garbage; indeed, when possible, we strongly recommend donating, giving away, or reselling what you no longer use, but in some cases, the only possible answer, unfortunately, is the garbage nerd!

Everything at once

KonMari's method is unforgiving: it is best to apply it all at once, even if this means taking the entire day.

Postponing or dividing the method into too many phases would seem the best way to fail. And if Madame Marie Kondo says so, who are we to contradict her?

Clothes

How many clothes have been sitting in the closet for months, if not years? In addition to the clothes, even those socks that have been unmatched for months, the underwear with the now gone elastics, scarves that we last put on back in 2005… everything away.

Only clothes worn regularly in the Spring / Summer and Autumn / Winter seasons should remain in the wardrobe. Everything else must disappear.

How you fold and hang your clothes is also essential,

Books

We like full bookcases and houses overflowing with books. Still, over the years, we risk accumulating many titles that we will never read again, and that only takes away space, collecting dust.

The used book market, for example, is very active, but associations, literary clubs, bookcrossing, and libraries can also be good choices to "free" the books that we no longer need.

Sheets, slips, scattered papers

The great enemies of clutter pop up in all corners of the house, from the desk to the bookcases, from the fridge to the drawers. Old receipts, photocopies, flying notes, and printed lists are all things we haven't looked at for months, making the house and our lives more messy and crowded.

In this case, no mercy; the important thing is to save the essential documents, and the rest must be thrown away.

Komono

The collection is perhaps the most complicated part to fix because it encompasses everything.

Everyone knows what brings disorder into their home; the important thing is to keep in mind another piece of advice that is part of the KonMari method: before putting everything back in order, immediately throw away all the discarded things, avoiding accumulating them in the garage or a box. !

CHAPTER 23

THE RULES TO FOLLOW TO PERFORM DECLUTTERING AT BEST

Have you ever felt suffocated in the house due to all the objects in every room that create disorder?

Do not worry; it is a sensation familiar to many: homes are often excessively full of objects that risk-taking over and create chaos that can generate a feeling of discomfort and throw you into despair.

In a conscious and reasoned way, the secret is to eliminate all we have accumulated over time, which is useless or does not represent something necessary. The way you organize your space can therefore affect, both positively and negatively, your state of mind and your mood. For this reason, it is essential to living in a tidy and organized home, and decluttering can help.

Especially if we want to embrace the wabi-sabi philosophy

BUT WHAT IS DECLUTTERING?

Literally, "to declutter" means "to make an order," so the word "decluttering" is often translated with the definition "to remove things you do not need from a place, to make it more pleasant and more useful." It is, therefore, the ability to make room and get rid of the extra.

It is a powerful weapon to improve your life and well-being and make you master your space and time again: by learning to get rid of the extra, you will immediately feel better and in a good mood.

1. THINGS TO KNOW BEFORE YOU BEGIN:

Decluttering requires a good dose of decision and the ability to live with small moments of melancholy and nostalgia. While you make room and get rid of the extra, you also come to terms with memories and the past. For this reason, decluttering involves not only the physical space but also the interior one.

You don't need to hurry to do everything right away, but proceed step by step according to the time available: you can choose whether to dedicate half an hour a day to decluttering or do everything over the weekend.

Don't move deleted things to the attic or basement - for decluttering to make sense, the things you don't need must be eliminated.

The decluttering process should not be seen as deprivation but as a fun and creative journey towards a regained simplicity.

2. HOW TO RECOGNIZE A SUPERFLUOUS OBJECT?

This is the focal point of the whole process. The first few times, it may seem complicated, but slowly you will be able to recognize different objects on the fly. Look at each item in the room you are tidying up, and ask yourself:

1. if you still like it.

2. if it is applicable.

3. if it has sentimental value.

Any item that does not meet these three criteria must be put aside. Do not keep an object just because your mother gave it to you and you think she would be upset if she didn't see it anymore or because "one day" it might come in handy: if you haven't used it so far, it means that you can make it. Unless forever.

Decluttering means just that: getting rid of the extra and tidying up. The idea of living a simpler life with fewer material things interests many, but they often find themselves not knowing where to start and asking themselves many questions, such as:

"What if I still need this object?". As we said before, if you haven't used it until now, you can do without it.

"Isn't it bad to throw away things that still work?". You don't have to throw them away - you can give them away, sell them or donate them to charity, but more on that later!

The wardrobe is the perfect example: how many useless clothes do we tend to accumulate without realizing it? How many clothes do we wear? Take it all out, choose and then decide what to donate and throw away. Some shops take old clothes back in exchange for shopping vouchers.

112

Here are some examples of items to delete:

- Dry cleaners hangers

- Sports gadgets

- Tablecloths too large or small

- Mismatched socks

- Unnecessary business cards

- Souvenirs you don't like

- Stained, torn, or frayed towels

- Obsolete video games

- Notebooks that are no longer needed

- Store catalogs available online

- Ruined clothes

- Broken electronic appliances

- Cookbooks you've never used

- Shoes that hurt are old or are worn out

- Broken toys or board games with missing pieces

- Dishes you never use

- Greeting cards, wedding invitations, etc.

- Old calendars

- Empty shoeboxes

- Boxes of electronic devices whose warranty has expired

- chargers and old cables of various types

- Unused or damaged backpacks and bags

- Decorative elements (favors) that you no longer like

- Cosmetics that are out of date or you don't like and nail polishes that have congealed

- Damaged or unworn jewelry (e.g., mismatched earrings, broken necklaces)

And here's why you won't miss these things:

They are old: you will never wonder why you have thrown away all those unused cables or those uncomfortable shoes.

They're broken - if you wanted to fix those things, you would have already done so.

You and your beloved family no longer need - this is the most important thing.

3. HOW TO ORGANIZE THE DECLUTTERING

There are two unique ways you can take, depending on how you are best at the organizational level:

1st method: go to rooms.

2nd method: go for types of products.

Go for rooms

It is the most straightforward system to follow because it allows you to work on something targeted: choose the room to arrange and work on it until you have obtained the desired result.

How to organize the work?

Take out everything you want to analyze (for example, all the clothes in the closet) and place it on a free surface.

At this point, divide all the objects by choosing whether to keep them, throw them away or give them away.

After a thorough cleaning of the spaces, put away the objects to keep organizing them as best suited to your needs.

It is essential to put away everything used regularly and instead set what is used only occasionally in the most uncomfortable places. Using suitable quality boxes and baskets will help keep things clean and tidy more efficiently and put things away quickly once used. Finally, it is beneficial to use labels when storing something rarely used.

To simplify the process, you can divide it into two stages. You'll be sure you want to delete some items, but you may have some doubts about others. Then put all the objects in "maybe" in a box or bag. At the end of the selection and first elimination work, you will have a clearer idea of the usefulness of keeping something of what you have provisionally placed in the box. You will be able to act in consequence.

Proceed in this way room by room until you have completed the whole house.

A little trick: to keep your clothes tidy, buy some fabric boxes (you can buy them from Ikea or online) and put away the clothes. If you roll them up, they won't have creases when you take them out to put them on!

Go for types of products.

It is the most complicated system since not all clothing is in the bedroom wardrobes in the house, electronic equipment is not all in the same room, and ornaments, books, magazines, etc.

Going for products means examining the whole house by focusing on a particular product (example: electronic equipment) and acting on it. The work is undoubtedly more complex, but it offers better results in many cases.

Look for all the objects of a specific category and store them, if you can, to always know where they are. In this case, all the accessories and phone chargers have been kept in small Ikea Godmorgon containers - it's a very clever idea for organizing drawers.

DECLUTTERING: KEEPING THE "MEMORIES" YES OR NO?

Most of the objects we have at home do not serve a specific task but are part of the "memory" of the life of one's family: I'm talking about letters, photo albums, objects dear to our ancestors, and much more. In this case, the choice is personal and must be made after careful reflection on the importance that specific memories can have in family life.

4. WHAT TO DO WITH THE OBJECTS TO BE ELIMINATED?

Donating to Associations: I always recommend donating to local charities and organizations as much as possible. Presenting what you don't need is twice as good: you'll have fewer things in your home, and other people will get the items they need.

A gift to those you know: if you know that relatives or friends need something that you own and no more prolonged use, but it is in good condition, give it to them: from clothes put on once and never again to equipment for children (seats, cots, etc..), anything that can help them will be seen as a very welcome gift.

Resell: if you have any valuables you don't use (jewelry, appliances, silverware, etc.), you can always resell them online or in thrift markets. If you want to get rid of antique furniture, call an antique dealer for an appraisal to know their exact price.

Throw away: Finally, don't feel guilty if many things, especially if broken, end up in the trash. Always remember: your home is not a warehouse. Some things must be thrown away, adopting the most appropriate system from time to time: undifferentiated or differentiated garbage for small and medium-sized objects, while landfills for larger objects and household appliances. Remember to respect the environment!

SPECIAL MENTION: THE DECLUTTERING OF BOOKS

A necessary premise: books should never be thrown away for any reason. So, if you need to make room in the library or your house is too crowded with books, the keyword is: give as a gift.

Among the possible recipients of the books you have discarded: are neighborhood libraries, schools, hospitals, retirement homes, prisons, and other types of communities.

5. THE TRICK OF THE BAG

This is a little trick you can use to keep your house tidy after you have it fixed or before doing an initial roughing:

Get a bag.

Decide what to focus on (Paper? Plastic? Other?).

Take a tour of the whole house.

Throw everything that is too much into the bag without thinking about it so much. Do not put it on hold when it is complete: get out of the house immediately and throw everything away. How do you feel? Do you feel a feeling of relief and lightness?

The secret to the success of this system is only one: zero organization.

It's so simple it can't fail.

It is perfect for giving a packed house a first "blow."

It gives a feeling of relief and success instantly and with little effort.

It is very effective as a maintenance technique.

118

It can be applied in the vast majority of situations.

The technique has its limits: it cannot take you alone to "solve" an entire house, but to make skimming and set a decluttering that seems stuck to the starting grids, the bag trick is ideal. What do you think about it?

Try to go by material: so you can use a plastic bag for all plastic objects, a paper bag for sheets and documents, and to simplify the recycling of materials!

FINALLY, A TIDY AND LIVABLE HOUSE!

When the job is done, you will be surprised to discover a more spacious house, where everything has its place, and there are no piles of unused objects.

But how do you keep the results over time?

Pay attention to making purchases aware that they do not go to fill your house with unnecessary items again.

To adopt this little rule, one must go out for everything that enters.

Use the bag trick frequently to avoid the new accumulation of items.

But I'm sure that once this hard work is done, you will have no desire to return to your old messy and stuffy house: the satisfaction of being surrounded only by beautiful objects that represent us will be stronger than any form of laziness!

And now, a roundup of ideas for ordering your home after throwing away the extra elements!

Bathroom idea / 1: if you have a drawer, organize it with small boxes to divide the various products: in this way, everything will have its place, and you will not waste time looking for things. You can find dividers online.

Bathroom idea / 2: No problem if you have doors instead of drawers. Store the products in baskets, better if made specifically for the organization than divided internally.

Wardrobe idea / 1: for the drawers, use dividers to find everything on the fly!

Wardrobe idea / 2: instead of folding sweaters and T-shirts, roll them up on themselves so as not to create creases and to optimize space.

Closet idea / 3: To organize the closet, you can use boxes. This will facilitate the organization and the change of season: just swap the boxes with the clothes of the past season with the boxes of the current one.

Kitchen idea / 1: to make the most of the space, use risers.

Kitchen idea / 2: make the most of the space under the sink by using containers for bulkier products and a basket to hang on the door for smaller products.

Kitchen idea / 3: even in the refrigerator, use containers to separate the various products and keep everything in order.

CHAPTER 24

KINTSUGI THE JAPANESE TECHNIQUE THAT TRANSFORMS BROKEN CERAMIC OBJECTS REPAIRED WITH GOLD INTO ART

When a plate, a vase, or a bowl breaks, shattering into a thousand pieces, albeit with regret, we throw them away. However, we should take an example from the Japanese, who practice the kintsugi technique for some ceramic and porcelain objects, a repair system using resin and gold dust that highlights cracks and fractures instead of being invisible.

Kintsugi, the Japanese art of repairing cracks with gold, increasing their value

Kintsugi mean

Literally, in Japanese, it means 'to repair with gold.' The union of the two words kin means 'to reunite' or 'to repair,' and tsugi, which means 'reunion.' It is also sometimes found as kin-tsukuroi.

In practice, this technique adds value to the broken object. But it is not just a repair; it is also a philosophy of life. The underlying concept can also have a profound symbolic meaning.

It is a technique and also a philosophy of Japanese origin. Like other practical forms that hide deep meanings linked to oriental philosophy, such as Ikebana, the art of arranging flowers, ikigai, the search for one's self, or the Zen garden, kintsugi also has a Zen implication.

It means 'to repair with gold' and is an ancient Japanese technique that repairs ceramic and porcelain objects, such as vases, plates, and trays, using gold to weld the various fragments together.

The cracks thus remain evident and not hidden, as we Westerners would be led to believe when it comes to repairing a broken object. And indeed, it increases its value.

Origins, history, and legend of kintsugi

It is a restoration technique devised at the end of the 15th century by Japanese potters to repair the delicate porcelain cups for the tea ceremony.

Legend has it that Ashikaga Yoshimasa, VIII Shogun of the Ashikaga Shogunate, after breaking his favorite cup, sent it to China to have it repaired.

Since the repairs of the time were done with metallic ligatures that were not very beautiful from an aesthetic point of view, Ashikaga Yoshimasa decided to try the repair again by contacting some Japanese craftsmen.

These, surprised by the shogun's tenacity in getting his beloved cup back, decided to try to transform it into a sort of jewel, filling the cracks with lacquered resin and gold dust.

The kintsugi technique

The traditional technique foresees that the broken pieces of the ceramic object are welded together with a thin layer of urushi lacquer, which is derived from the resin of a tree.

First plastered and then sanded, the breaking lines are finished with red urushi lacquer with a brush on which the gold dust is dropped.

The purpose of this type of repair is not to hide the damage but to emphasize it, incorporating it into the aesthetics of the repaired object.

From an artistic point of view, the repaired piece will thus be "better" than the new object and will be considered more precious, both for the presence of gold or silver and for its uniqueness.

The breaking lines joined with urushi lacquer are left visible and more highlighted with gold dust.

The ceramic objects repaired with this artistic technique become true works of art. Their fragility is transformed into a point of strength and perfection. Each repaired ceramic presents a different intertwining of unique and unrepeatable golden lines due to the randomness with which the ceramic can be shattered.

This practice stems from the idea that an even greater form of aesthetic and interior perfection can be born from imperfection and a wound.

What it takes to do the Kintsugi

The material used as the glue is urushi lacquer, which is extracted from the native Rhus plant Verniciflua. But rice or wheat flour, Tomoko, and gold and silver dust are also used.

The drying process of the lacquer, used as an adhesive for ceramic, a stucco, and as an adhesive for gold dust, takes place in the wall, in a warm environment (about 25 °) and with a relative humidity of around 70- 80%. The drying time is variable: it ranges from 3 to 7 days.

The philosophy of kintsugi

This is not only a mere artistic concept but also has deep roots in Zen philosophy. The concepts enclosed would be:

Mushin: the ability to let go, forget worries, and free the mind from pursuing perfection.

Anicca or impermanence: the awareness of fate and the transience of existence. All things are destined to end, and we must accept this condition with a calm and conscious approach.

Mono no - aware: a kind of empathy for objects. Appreciating its decadence, one comes to admire its beauty.

This ancient art of repairing precious objects is often used as a symbol and metaphor for the concept of resilience.

Furthermore, it would also represent the concept of fracture in a broad sense and, therefore, the crises and changes that the individual may have to face in life.

The basic idea is that a better and even more effective form of perfection, aesthetic and interior, can be born from imperfection and a wound.

In this practice, the broken vase or object is repaired without hiding the cracks, but, on the contrary, the latter is especially emphasized through a precious material such as gold. This enhancement of the fracture represents the new history of the broken object.

The idea of recovering and enhancing an object that otherwise would have lost its intended use can also be applied to people. Even after a break or damage, it is possible to overcome and 'heal' one's internal wounds and become better.

And again, as the precious metal enhances the fractures, the person can proudly show his scars because they represent his experience in the process of rebirth.

What can it do today?

In this period, in particular, many of us need tranquility, free the mind for a moment from the hectic thoughts of the day, and worry-free. Right now, even very normal activities such as shopping, which we are usually used to doing since childhood, for many bring with it anxiety and stress.

However, a hobby that could be started is that of Kintsugi, albeit in a small way. To glue the pieces together takes a lot of concentration (so much so that Japanese artists who practice this technique sometimes take more than a month to repair a single object), so the mind has to concentrate only on this, letting go of the rest and fixing itself in one dimension of calm.

With what to practice it?

Top-rated is specific kits, which can be purchased in specialized shops for DIY and the restoration of antique objects or online to proceed and practice this ancient technique with the right tools. To learn the method and find inspiration for a new creation, you can consult various texts.

CHAPTER 25

HOW TO DO THE KINTSUGI

T he traditional technique is very complex and challenging to reproduce, especially since it is not so easy to find urushi lacquer.

We can perform kintsugi-style ceramic repairs using cutting-edge materials thanks to modern synthetic resin technology.

Furthermore, to carry out an inexpensive operation, it is possible to replace real gold and silver with metallic pigments that imitate the features of the two precious items.

At this point, it is time to move on to practice. Let's see what we need and how to proceed to repair a broken object with this technique:

- object in ceramic or porcelain

- two-component epoxy glue

- gold or silver powder or simple metallic pigments

- chopsticks to mix the various components

- brush for finishing

Preparation. Mix the two-component glue with the gold powder or imitation pigments in a bowl. Consider three parts of glue for one metal powder.

Assemble the various fragments trying to respect the original arrangement. Spread a sufficient and homogeneous amount of adhesive paste on the edge of the piece. Keep the parts glued in place for a few minutes to facilitate fixing. And repeat the operation with all the fragments.

Using a brush, go over the gluing so that the material expands well, even outside the crack of the break. By doing so, the repair will take on a deep gold or silvery color.

It is essential not to remove the golden glue from the joint. This is precisely the peculiar characteristic of this repair technique.

If some small ceramic pieces are missing, we can fill the gaps with epoxy glue mixed with the metal powder.

Finally, it is also possible to avoid mixing the epoxy glue with the metal powder, simply gluing the fragments only with great glue. At the end of the gluing operations, rain a sufficient quantity of metal powder onto the excess adhesive that comes out of the joints.

What glue to use for kintsugi

Lacquer should be used, but regular two-component epoxy glue to mix with gold powder is fine.

It should be applied abundantly to the ceramic cracks to remain visible along with the damage from the joints.

Also known as kintsukuroi, it is the Japanese technique that repairs broken ceramic objects with gold.

And that invites us to love and show imperfections (even ours)!

REQUIRED

- two-component glue

- golden powder

- some chopsticks to mix the components

- brush for finishing

HOW TO DO

- Mix the two-component glue with the gold powder

- Apply the mixture obtained to the ceramic cracks so that it is abundant and visible

- Hold the parts to be glued in place for a few minutes

- With a brush, carefully go over the gluing so that the material spreads well even outside the crack of the break and the repair takes on intense gold color.

CHAPTER 26

HOW TO RECOVER OLD LAMPSHADES

Do you have a lamp you adore, but whose lampshade you hate? Or maybe you've remodeled a room recently and want the lights to match the rest but don't want to break the piggy bank to buy all new lamps? Whatever your reasons, getting your lampshades back is your best bet. You need an old lampshade, some new fabric, and a little creativity.

1-Take measures

Prepare your work table. It will be better to work on a table because you will need a flat surface on which you can arrange all your materials. Place newspaper on the table and the floor around your countertop, as the spray adhesive can stick to almost any surface and could damage your furniture or beds.

2-Remove the old fabric from the shape of the lampshade. Remove the hem (if there is one) by pulling it. The scissors pierce the old material and cut pieces off the body. Do not cut the lining fabric.

Depending on the adhesive used to adhere the fabric to the shape, you may be able to cut sections and then use your fingers to pull the remaining pieces of material off the frame cord.

3-Spread out a piece of pattern paper and measure your lampshade. Make sure the article is flat and wrinkle-free. Roll the lampshade in the report, tracing the edges it forms with a pencil. To get an exact measurement, it is essential to track where you started on the lamp.

4-Add length to the shape you drew. You will need some extra fabric, so you should add 1.5cm along both long sides of the body you removed from your lampshade and 2.5cm to one of the short sides.

5-Cut the pattern paper along the lines you created. You will use this template as a stencil for the shape you cut from your fabric.

6-Choose your fabric. When retrieving a lampshade, choose the light, relatively thin material.

Consider the design of the fabric. While lamps with a top and bottom of equal sizes will work well with any material, lights with a small shelter and broad base will look odd wrapped in a vertical line pattern (which tends to appear to fall into the back seam).

Cut the fabric

1- Ensure there are no wrinkles or creases and that the material is completely smooth on the flat surface. You need to spread it out so you don't accidentally cut it into a fold and end up with an asymmetrical fabric cover for your lampshade.

2-Spread your pattern on the fabric. Make sure the paper is flat too. You can use pins to keep it snug against the material.

3-Mark the back of the material. Using a suitable pen or some other drawing tool that you will be able to see on the fabric, trace the outline of the paper stencil. Be very careful to be as accurate as possible. You draw on the back of the material to make sure that the drawing does not show on the final result.

4-Cut out the material. Using fabric scissors, gently cut the material along the lines created with the fabric pen. Remove any remaining fabric from the work area.

Retrieve the lampshade

1-Spray your fabric with adhesive. It is essential to do this in a well-ventilated area, as the spray adhesive can be harmful if you breathe in too much. Remember that adhesive spray is incredibly sticky (and permanent), so make sure you don't put it on anything beyond the fabric.

If you bought an adhesive-backed fabric, you do not need to use spray adhesive on the material. Use the adhesive canvas to adhere the fabric to the shape of the lampshade. You must first heat the canvas with an iron, place it in place on the body, and finally cover the canvas with the fabric. Spread the material as you move it around the sides of the canvas and shape it until the lampshade is wholly protected.

2-Place your lamp and add the fabric. To do this, center the lampshade in the material so that the edge of the fabric and the existing seam of the lampshade are aligned. Roll the lampshade along with the fabric, stretching the fabric and removing any creases.

If you are using a fabric with a design, it is also essential to make sure the design lines up correctly when attaching the material to the lampshade.

3-Create a seam with the extra fabric on the short side (the vertical edge). You'll have additional material to roll your lampshade into. Rather than leaving the edge of the fabric visible, fold the excess fabric to create a straight hem. Make sure you only use a little glue - if you use too much, it may come off the hem (which isn't the best to see).

4-To give your lampshade a finished look, it is best to fold the extra material inside the lampshade. Make sure it stays up and down by securing it with hot glue.

5-Add some finishing touches. To make your lampshade look fresh from the shop, add a coating along the bottom edge of the lamp. Simply use hot glue to attach a thicker piece of fabric along the top and bottom edges of your light. You can also add some fringe, a rick-rack hem, or other materials to cover the top and bottom edges of the lampshade with its new coating.

Advice

To make this project even cheaper, look for old lamps at thrift markets.

Things you will need:

- Lampshade

- Scissors

- Fabric

- Tape measure

- Line

- Pencil for fabrics

- Spray adhesive

- Iron (if using material with an adhesive side)

- Hot glue

CHAPTER 27

SHIBORI: HOW TO DYE AND NATURALLY DECORATE FABRICS WITH THE ANCIENT JAPANESE TECHNIQUE

S hibori is an ancient Japanese technique for dyeing fabrics still little known in the West. In shibori, cloths are tied and manipulated or protected in other ways before being immersed in the dye bath.

Shibori is an ancient Japanese technique for dyeing fabrics still little known in the West. In shibori, cloths are tied and manipulated or protected in other ways before being immersed in the dye bath.

In this type of dyeing, very particular decorations are obtained. The parts of the fabric that do not have to absorb the color are protected to make this happen. It is interesting to experiment with this technique using vegetable dyes obtained from plants and vegetables (for example, beet, wisteria, or nettle).

With this technique, very original abstract decorations are obtained. This technique comes from the word " shibori, "which means to twist, tighten and press. Similar dyeing techniques in India and other countries such as Malaysia and Indonesia have different names, such as banda and trick.

Compared to the more well-known " tie and dye techniques, "much more imaginative, rich and varied decorations are obtained with shibori.

- Materials

- 100% cotton fabrics

- Powder dyeing for fabrics or suitable vegetable dyes

- Clothes pegs, rubber bands, office clips

- Twine

- Wooden dowels and sticks of various sizes

- Waterproof gloves

1) Prepare the color in a pot or bucket. You can try experimenting with natural dyes with vegetables, flowers, and leaves. Read here.

2) Cut out a square of fabric from the chosen cotton fabric. Test with a square with a side of 45 cm. Most shibori techniques suggest starting with a square shape.

3) Fold the fabric back on itself to obtain a triangle from your square. Or fold the fabric like an accordion to make a rectangle.

4) Secure the folded fabrics with wooden sticks and rubber bands and clothes pegs, and document clips. Also, place oval and square wooden dowels on the fabric parts you would like to decorate in a

particular way and secure them with rubber bands.

5) Secure folded fabrics very well using rubber bands and clothes pegs. Put on waterproof gloves and dip the materials in the dye bath. The more the fabric remains immersed, the more intense the color will be.

6) For powder dyes for fabrics, a time of 45 minutes can be respected, but always check the instructions on the package carefully. For natural dyes, longer times may be needed. Some powder dyes may require adding calcium carbonate to the dye bath.

7) Remove the fabrics from the dye bath after the rest time. Rinse them very well, and then let them dry.

CHAPTER 28
HOW TO MAKE A SCREEN YOURSELF

Wooden screen for the house: how to make it yourself. Useful DIY ideas.

A practical and excellent idea for furnishing the house and organizing spaces can be to use booths or dividers. There are many on the market, in wood with rigid panels, with slats or shutters, or in fabric, plain or printed, on a wooden frame.

On the market, in furniture stores, there are many. You have to choose the one that's right for you. Or you can make your booth yourself—an opportunity to learn how to create something new and have a lot of satisfaction.

Wooden screen for the house: how to make it yourself

The easiest way to make wooden screens is to get boards that have already been cut or have them cut to size. Or cut them yourself if you are experienced in carpentry. Once you have your panels, you can leave them in natural wood or paint them if you get by with paint. A surefire decoration is the one that involves the use of stencil and découpage techniques. Once the decoration is finished, join the panels of your booth with particular hinges, which you will apply after making small holes in the wood where you can insert the screws. You can let the base of your booth panels touch the ground if it is thick and stable enough, or you can apply feet to the floor.

Instead of panels, you can prepare or have a wooden frame designed, with or without feet. In the empty spaces, inside the squares or rectangles of the frame, insert the fabric of your choice taut, fixing it on the back with wood glue or small staples to be applied with the appropriate stapler.

Screen in Japanese wood

Finally, an original and refined idea can create a Japanese shoji booth. These dividers are widely used in Japanese homes, both as screens and as natural walls, doors, or sliding doors. They have a square frame made of light-colored light wood. At the same time, the spaces inside the structure are covered with fine Japanese paper. You will already find wooden strips and Japanese paper in stores specializing in DIY and home DIY.

Once you have purchased the necessary, mount the wooden strips according to the size of the screen and the number of panels you want to make. The strips of the external frame will be thicker for the stability and solidity of the structure. At the same time, the internal ones are lighter. You can also make a single ample panel rest on wooden feet for stability. Or you can also apply wheels to the base.

To form the structure of the Japanese screen, join the various wooden strips with small nails, the groups to be applied with a not too heavy hammer. Make square frames. Then, in the empty spaces of the squares, use the Japanese paper to be fixed to the strips, at the back of the screen, with glue or staples, as above. Join the panels with the hinges. You can create quadrangular support bases to be arranged diagonally to fold the meetings for more excellent stability. Indeed, the wooden feet or the wheels allow greater mobility to the boards, which you can also tuck into a booklet when you want to put away your screen.

The Japanese shoji screen is elegant and highly versatile. It allows you to hope for the environments of the same room with discretion, without weighing down the furniture, and above all, it gives excellent brightness thanks to the lightness of the Japanese paper that lets the light filter through.

CHAPTER 29
CONCLUSIONS

T rends in interior design are constantly changing. Today wabi design has come to the fore Sabi. It refers to minimalism, vanishing, and a lack of attachment to material objects.

Wabi-Sabi originates in the Land of the Rising Sun - Japan. On the other hand, Sabi is an artistic term that can be translated as covering things with the patina of time. The Wabi-Sabi definition refers to a style philosophy of finding beauty in humble and not quite perfect things.

A reference to nature and simplicity can characterize Wabi-Sabi design. Without a doubt, natural materials are its most essential elements:

- natural wood

- stone

- wicker

It is better if these materials are marked with use. As for the decorations, Wabi-Sabi art is dominated by ceramics, such as small candle holders and vases.

Wabi-Sabi design – colors:

- beige

- dark or light brown

- shades of gray

- white

Due to the colors referring to the earth, the Wabisabi interior looks significantly warmer and more welcoming. Plus, they make the room seem bigger. It is essential for interiors with little space, for example, a small living room or bedroom.

The neutral colors on the walls also promote quick relaxation, for example, after a long day at work. One can calm down and sleep in such an interior.

Wabi-Sabi - characteristic materials:

The meaning of Wabi Sabi also refers to the non-attachment to the quality of the products.

When choosing fabrics, it is recommended to choose linen. This material wrinkles easily, so accessories made with it always look crumbled - it fits perfectly into the Wabi-Sabi design.

The philosophy is also about evanescence and the passing of time - the wear and tear of the furniture used in the interiors.

An interesting effect can be achieved by using a unique method that makes the plaster look like it is falling off.

Wabi-Sabi design - for which interiors is it suitable?

Wabi-Sabi's design looks good in any interior. But you have to accept the passage of time - the gradual damage to furniture and other objects. Lack of attachment to new items is key to this style, so it might be good to look for second-hand furniture with a fascinating history and age. ** Currently, many manufacturers offer custom furniture collections for the Japanese philosophy.

Wabi-Sabi design – accessories:

Wabi-Sabi art and philosophy refer to nature. A piece of bark with some moss and a few small candles could be a good decoration. Even a single flower in a small vase matches this style perfectly.

You can also make perfect decorations using the DIY method - for example, a candle holder.

Wabi-sabi art, fabrics:

Authenticity is also the watchword for fabrics.

Space for natural alternatives such as wool, linen, and organic cotton is even better if with raw and material processing. Greenlight for a thick-weave plaid or tricot to be placed at the foot of the bed, on an armchair, or on the sofa, ready to give warmth and comfort.

On the other hand, unpressed linen sheets are the protagonists of a bed not made to perfection.

Natural and non-ironed fabrics characterize wabi-sabi.

We also find linen in the kitchen. A tablecloth or runner made with this material gives character to a table embellished with a vase of wildflowers and a freshly baked cake to be enjoyed alone or in good company during a sweet afternoon break.

And for a break that involves all the senses, how about letting yourself be enveloped by the soft embrace of an organic cotton bathrobe to wear after a nice warm bath?

Relaxation will be guaranteed.

Wabi-sabi art, colors

The sense of natural imperfection that characterizes wabi-sabi art also influences the choice of colors. Which ones to bet on? Indicate the palettes that run through earth tones, alternating with warm and versatile whites.

But not only that: wabi-sabi culture is contemplation and acceptance of things. Therefore, it is normal for it to be associated with a meditative lifestyle that prefers not very bright shades.

In this sense, the furnishings that include the whole scale of grays and intense blues on cushions, textiles, sheets, and small objects should be enhanced.

To give the house a personal touch of color, we can use floral solutions, such as lavender, placed in recycled vases; a cast iron teapot with an oriental allure is perfect.

Let's not forget, then, to recreate an even more intimate atmosphere with soft lights to be placed at strategic points of the house.

We have seen so far the materials, fabrics, and nuances that characterize the wabi-sabi style, but how do we propose them in various domestic environments?

The common thread is functional and aesthetic essentiality; spaces must be comfortable and sober, transmitting inner harmony.

To embellish the relaxation area or the reading corner, accessories and decorations with simple lines and a recycled look include jute rugs, rattan baskets, and bamboo lampshades.

However, the focus shifts to the mise en place in the kitchen or the dining room.

The table is dressed in delicacy and is tinged with natural shades: a linen or cotton tablecloth, recycled glass bottles as vase holders, and sets of plates and glasses that combine different patterns and materials. And then, a chipped plate can find its place next to a perfectly intact one.

Wabi-sabi touch to the bedroom.

Rattan abat-jour, a set of raw cotton percale sheets, invites us to enjoy a good rest. A pile of books and magazines still to be read can be transformed into an unusual table.

In general, a room must be thought of as a place that invites rest and concentration.

Its essentially minimalist character induces us to dispense with furniture that is not strictly necessary. After all, getting rid of what you don't use is undoubtedly a way of simplifying your life.

The idea of the Japanese style is based on simplicity and cleanliness (there is just a term to indicate a room furnished with the Japanese style: Washitsu).

An inevitable element in the bedrooms and, if desired, in the other rooms is the booth shoji, a folding panel usually made of rice paper and bamboo or wood. It is a traditional element of Japanese culture when it comes to furnishings.

The booths shoji can help hide things and objects that we have in a room, such as the living room, where we usually receive guests, and that we do not want to be in sight, such as, for example, cardboard boxes or gym bags.

But be careful when you ask for shoji: formally, shoji means both room dividers (Akari shoji) and the sliding doors inside the rooms, fusuma (also called kirigami shoji), and the windows made with blown rice paper, lighter than fusuma to allow light to enter (which are called shoji).

If the view from the bedroom window is not to your liking, the people across the street are too close; the shoji panels can be placed in front of the window to protect your privacy while allowing light to filter through. And light up the room.

It is preferable to choose low furniture that allows more significant space.

Of Japanese conception are also zabuton, zafu, and futon.

Replacing the summer mattress with a futon is a choice that is economically advantageous and allows you to save space.

The choice of colors must fall on neutral colors. Japanese decoration is based on balance.

Wooden furniture and a slightly brighter color focused on a single point of the room, for example, the bed, are indicated, breaking the neutral colors' motor.

The sheets and curtains could be silk, a fabric that goes well with a Japanese décor.

Finally, always remember the golden rule less is more.

CPSIA information can be obtained
at www.ICGtesting.com
Printed in the USA
BVHW052300300623
666613BV00011B/968